The
Lighthouse Keeper

The
Lighthouse Keeper

How To Be The Guiding Light For Your Children
As You Help Prepare Them For Their Journey Through Life

By Carol Kitchin

XULON PRESS

Xulon Press
2301 Lucien Way #415
Maitland, FL 32751
407.339.4217
www.xulonpress.com

Unless otherwise indicated, Scripture quotations taken from the Holy Bible,
New International Version (NIV). Copyright © 1973, 1978, 1984, 2011 by
Biblica, Inc.™. Used by permission. All rights reserved.

Printed in the United States of America

Paperback ISBN-13: 978-1-6628-1468-6

Dedication

~◦~

*T*his book is dedicated to my family who have been patient with me as I have learned to embrace the role of wife, mother, and grandmother. My husband Lloyd has been my solid ground since I first met him when I was 16 years old and he believes that there is nothing that I can't accomplish. My children bring me my greatest pride and joy as I have watched them learn to navigate their own boats and I now have the joy of watching them successfully guide their own children.

I want to thank my precious daughter Jessica for editing this book and using her expertise in writing to help her mom. Thanks to my friends who have been my sounding board and loyal supporters throughout the many decades of my life, and to my many spiritual leaders that have taught me the value of a strong faith and the peace that comes from having a relationship with God. I am blessed to know you. And lastly, to my sister, Kathy, whom I lost when I was only 18 years old. Her journey to heaven strengthened my faith and led me to have a lifetime journey with my heavenly Father. I am comforted in knowing that one day we will be reunited.

C arol Kitchin is a wife, mother, grandmother, nurse, and educator. She has been married to her husband, Lloyd, since 1981 and together they have four children: one daughter and three sons. Currently she is blessed with nine grandchildren. She lives in the northwest section of New Jersey on Lake Hopatcong and has sailed competitively since she was 16 years old. She won the Thistle Women's National Championship as a crew and has won many sailing titles over her career. She ran the Junior Sailing program at Lake Hopatcong Yacht Club for five years and is still actively sailing with her husband and occasionally with her children. She is a registered nurse who has worked at Saint Barnabas Medical Center in Livingston, N.J., for 40 years and was head nurse of Maternity. She currently teaches the maternity orientation, newborn classes, lamaze, and grand-parenting classes. She has been a substitute school nurse, director of a nursery school, leader of a parenting support group called "The Lighthouse Keepers," PTA president, confirmation leader, Sunday school teacher, Bible study leader, and president of many youth organizations. She was a Girl Scout leader for eight years and ran the church youth ski trips for 20 years along with chaperoning two trips to the National Youth organization in both New Orleans and San Antonio. She is still active in the local school by leading class trips to her boathouse for the town's second graders to talk about the local history, and on a monthly basis she speaks to the sixth-grade class in a program that she developed called "MAPS to the Future" where she teaches life skills such as cooking, finance, car repairs, and first aid. She also volunteers with the Lake Hopatcong Foundation and helps educate hundreds of students each year on their class trips. Her passion is education and helping new parents feel empowered to take on the new role of parenthood. She is fortunate to live close to most of her children and able to serve an active role in their lives. She also likes to ski, golf, bike, kayak, and, of course sail.

kitchinlighthouse@gmail.com

Chapters

1. What Does It Mean To Be A Lighthouse 1
2. The Lighthouse Stands Alone 9
3. The Light Shines Even In The Bright of Day 15
4. Calm Seas 25
5. Lifesavers 41
6. Prepare Them For The Journey 51
7. Putting Your Team Together 65
8. The Value Of The Compass 93
9. Don't Leave Shore Without Your Anchor 109
10. When To Bellow 121
11. Who Is Steering The Boat 135
12. Rocky Shores and Strong Currents 149
13. The Journey Home 165
14. Sending The Boats Out To Sea 179
15. What Happens After The Ship Sails 195
16. Enjoy The Ride 213

CHAPTER 1

What Does It Mean
To Be A Lighthouse?

———

What does it mean to be that tall immovable object that is found by rough seas or on rocky shores that guides passing ships and helps them avoid dangers, whose sole purpose is to safely guide unsuspecting boats away from danger and allow them to continue safely on their journey?

That is the role of a parent, to be a lighthouse that guides our children. We were entrusted with doing a valuable and important job when God blessed us with our children. When we held them as little babies and they completely trusted us for their very survival, we may not have fully understood the strength and wisdom that we were going to need for this job. They were helpless and unable to survive without the nurturing support of a caregiver who would see to all of their needs. That is what God intended. God created them and we are called to raise them. We are to be the link between our heavenly Father and the dangerous and unsettling world that our children live in. We need to provide food, clothing, safety, and love to this little being that has no means to help themselves. As caretakers, our God-given role is to guide them to become independent, self-sufficient, responsible adults; we are to be the guiding light that shines for them and leads them along a challenging and sometimes dangerous journey. To be their lighthouse.

As a lighthouse, we have the ability to warn them of approaching dangers such as jagged rocks and treacherous currents that may turn over their small craft. The beacon warns them of trouble that they may not see and our light may guide them away from the dangerous shoreline that can cause havoc to their tiny vessel. As parents we need to be attentive 24/7 so that they can see our light shining even on the darkest days. There may be times that we need to "bellow" or use the fog horn when they are surrounded by total darkness and can't see the way forward; our job is to draw attention to impending peril.

It is important to understand that our job is to guide them and be alert for trouble but it is not our job to get in their boat! This is their journey and they need to navigate the boat on their own. Our job is vital, we are the lighthouse that guides them on their travels and hopefully helps them stay away from trouble waters but the voyage is theirs. Our goal, and it's a big one, is to keep our light shining. We do little good if we allow our light to dim when the fog (especially during adolescence) comes rolling in. It is vital that we are sure- footed and a bright beacon for them to follow.

LIGHT

All too often I find that parents today allow their own lights to falter and even go out completely and then complain because their children have lost their way. When that happens both the child and the parent are drifting aimlessly and hoping that things will work out. If they are lucky, the current and winds may be favorable and cast their little boat away from the dangerous shores, but all too often — just when a child needs it the most — the lighthouse fails to shine and the boat is tossed up on the jagged rocks and destroyed at the foot of the lighthouse.

The goal of this book is to guide and inspire parents to regenerate their own light and allow them to shine brighter not only for their own children's sake but also for their own well-being. They should stand tall and bright and be a beacon for their children to follow. To be someone they can count on to "be there" when the world closes in on them and to help them travel on safely to the next port. Having a light to guide you can make the travel so much easier. Nothing is worse than to enter a dark room and be unable to find a light switch. You may bump into a table leg or trip on a shoe left in the middle of the room. Even though you have been in that room thousands of times, your sense of where things are becomes distorted. Unexpected items, such as a pair of shoes not put away properly may trip you up. You fumble and reach for anything that may illuminate your surroundings. As you search for a light switch, you may knock over things that normally wouldn't be in your way. You reach out for anything that feels familiar and shuffle slowly along a well-worn path. All the while you are searching for that switch that can light your way. Even a dim light is better than no light to help you on the journey and your children will feel the same way. They long to have you guide them and stand tall when they are feeling battered by the surf or lost at sea.

During Superstorm Sandy many people were without electricity for days and in some cases weeks. The common complaint was that they felt lost without the simple lights to guide them around their homes. They actually fought off depression as they searched for lights to guide them in their own homes. Familiar things seemed distorted and their bearings were off as soon as the sun went down. Simple acts such as meal preparation or getting dressed became stressful and the isolation of not being able to watch the news or knowing what was happening around them added to their anxiety.

The Lord has a better plan: He leaves the switch right by the door so we don't have to enter the darkened room where we may trip and fall. He encourages us daily to light our way so that simple trappings don't make us stumble. We can navigate around minor obstacles that could cause us to fall if we were in the dark. With God's light to guide us we can avoid stumbles that we may encounter along the way. We can have a clear path directing us where to go and we can be comforted knowing that someone is watching us and ready to help if we fall into danger.

The Bible is a reassurance of God's promises to us. I call the BIBLE my roadmap on how to get home. My guiding light that shows me the way and my **B**asic **I**nstruction **B**efore **L**eaving **E**arth.

In the Gospel of John, the Apostle tells us about the promise of Jesus lighting our way.

> **John 8:12** *When Jesus spoke again to the people, he said, "I am the light of the world. Whoever follows me will never walk in darkness, but will have the light of life."*

God wants us on a straight and narrow path that is always lit and well marked and that shows us the way home. He reminds us that we are just travelers on this journey and that our goal and the goal of parenting is to help everyone arrive safely home. To be able to hear the good Lord say, "Well done my good and faithful servant. Welcome home!"

> **Matthew 7:13** *Enter through the narrow gate. For wide is the gate and broad is the road that leads to destruction, and many enter through it. 14 But small is the gate and narrow the road that leads to life, and only a few find it.*

Parenting is tough and so is life. It is through God's words and promises that we are reminded over and over again that we aren't on this journey alone and we don't need to make this journey in the dark. The path that we will be traveling on is straight but narrow, so we will need to be in constant contact with our Heavenly Father to know that we are on track.

How often have you been up all night anxious and worried only to find in the morning, in the light of the day, that your fears were not as big as you thought? That the monster you were afraid of in the dark was nothing more than a carelessly discarded jacket thrown on a chair.

Light helps us find our way, casts away fears, and helps us avoid falls. Light can be the difference between a joy filled journey and one filled with anxiety and worry. As you look around, you can see people who seem to radiate light even during trials and those who always seem to be under a dark cloud. What is the difference and how can we live a life that is light filled? I know that every one of us could use a bit of more light in our lives and the way to get it is as simple as asking for it.

> **Matthew 7:7-8** *Ask, and it shall be given you;* **seek,** *and you shall find;* **knock,** *and the door will be opened: 8 For whoever asks, receives; and he that seeks shall find; and to him that knocks the door shall be opened.*

On this journey called life, we are cast in a boat and called to navigate the constantly changing conditions of the seas. I am a competitive sailor and have spent a lifetime learning to navigate the sailboat in all kinds of situations. There is a constant need to readjust, re-trim the sails, and reassess the wind direction. A race in a dying breeze can be just as challenging as the day with an impending storm. The weather can change in a moment's notice and the winds are in a constant state of flux. Navigating around a race course requires paying attention to wind shifts, being aware of your competitors, and working together in your boat to make it sail as fast as possible. As a team it is important to be on the same page and to have an understanding of how to make the boat travel smoothly through the constantly changing conditions. A successful team has the ability to see the whole picture and has an understanding that that picture is in a constant state of change.

The rudder is vital in a sailboat to guide the vessel, and even though it is small it is responsible for determining which direction you are going. If a boat loses its rudder, it becomes helpless and has no power to steer. It can't avoid the dangers of another boat or perhaps a rocky shoreline. It gets tossed by the waves and is at the mercy of the currents and winds of the day. It is unable to steer for itself and it is just praying to stay out of trouble.

Being able to navigate one's boat requires an understanding of how the boat works and how to manage the tiller that controls the rudder. When you first learn how to sail it is important to start in a small manageable boat that is slow moving and easy to steer. You can't progress to the fast sloop until you have an understanding of the mechanics of a smaller boat first. It requires baby steps to first get a feel of the boat and an understanding of the wind. As you become familiar with the dynamics of sailing you can progress to a faster and more challenging yacht. The training is important and the preparation vital before you leave the safety of the harbor. That is not unlike the importance of training a child before setting them off into the world. It is vital to equip them with the tools they need, stage by stage, to help them have the knowledge to navigate the open waters of life. By preparing them ahead of time, hopefully they will be equipped to handle what life throws their way. As a parent there is nothing that you want more than to keep your children safe, but on this life journey, at some point they need to leave the safety of the harbor and your job is to help them to be capable of navigating on their own. The goal is to help them to become young people of wisdom who have the tools needed to handle the turbulent waters that will come their way. To be able to know how to handle changing winds, turbulent waters, and unexpected breakdowns. To use the rudder to steer their boat in the proper direction. All of this takes years of training and preparation.

Pause for a moment and take a look back on your life and reflect on your childhood. Try to remember how secure you felt navigating your own boat. How prepared were you to set off on your own out into the open seas? Did you have to navigate a leaking ship or did your parents do a good job of securing your vessel before sending you out to face the open waters? Was your rudder (faith) secure and trustworthy or was it wobbly and loose and not completely able to turn away from dangers? Or perhaps you were you sent out to sea rudderless with no clear direction?

Were you guided on your journey with a compass that allowed you to know the direction home? If you sail in open waters it is vital to know the compass heading that will allow you to return back to the safety of the harbor and the security of home. If the fog comes in, or the wind dies and you can't make it to shore before dark, the only thing that allows you to know where to go is your compass. The compass will give you the confidence to be on the proper course and guide you when you cannot see. Life is like that, there will be times when you can't see where to go, but trusting in your compass (Jesus) to guide and help you will allow you to aim in the right direction and head for the safety of home.

As you reflect back perhaps your journey was an uneventful and joyous one. A journey filled with fond memories, loving family, and guiding parents. You were blessed because your parents were your lighthouse and prepared you properly for the journey. They stood tall on the hill and guided you, especially when the waters were rough. You felt unconditional love and had the power of a secure rudder and a dependable compass. Reflect on what a blessing you were given and use that model to empower your own children on their journey.

Maybe your childhood home wasn't as nurturing as you would have liked, but life was kind and instead of guiding parents, your vessel had the lifesaving power of a guiding compass or you were fortunate enough to encounter favorable seas and lifesaving currents that kept you out of harm's way. You didn't encounter many of the dangers of the world and so your journey kept you away from the dangerous shorelines that could have severely damaged your vessel. You can hope your children will be as lucky, but there is a risk in that.

If however, your journey has been rough and you felt rudderless, or without a compass to guide you and maybe you even crashed upon a few rocks along the shore, the good news is that you have the opportunity to change the legacy of the next generation. It isn't easy when you don't have the tools or the knowledge but just like sailing it can be learned and passed on.

To understand what you need to be a good lighthouse for your children and to help you give your kids the tools that they will need as they begin their journey is the goal of this book. It doesn't mean that your child won't hit rough seas, jagged shores and dangerous currents, but it will empower you to guide them as best you can. Hopefully, it will help you acquire wisdom and allow your light to shine brighter. It may be just the tool you need to give you peace during the storms and a sense of purpose as you guide your children. Sometimes the only hope for a vessel in dangerous waters can be a prayer for calmer seas and steady winds. That is where God comes in.

CHAPTER 2
The Lighthouse Stands Alone

━━━◦━━━

I f you have ever encountered a lighthouse you will notice that it usually stands alone against the backdrop of the sea. It stands tall against the landscape and is battered by the elements. Sometimes that is what it feels like to be a parent: battered by the circumstances in our lives, such as financial concerns, lack of time, peer pressures, and more, and yet as parents, just like a lighthouse, we have an important job to do. We are called to stand tall as the circumstances around us are battering our very foundation.

The lighthouse is vital for the survival of ships at sea as they approach an unknown and dangerous shoreline. The sea can be calm and steady or violent and unpredictable. It is when the sea poses dangerous conditions that a lighthouse needs to stand guard and warn the sailors to be alert and attentive to the potential of deadly consequences. While that lighthouse stands guard it can be battered by crashing waves, and stormy seas that wear upon the shoreline and undermines the foundation of the grand structure. Shifting sands can occur and slowly the entire structure can be off balanced and begin to crumble.

The greatest danger for a lighthouse is neglect. Back in the day when it was a manned tower the lighthouse keeper lovingly tended to the needs of the structure so that it would be prepared for the assaults of Mother Nature. Daily, he assessed the structure for any cracks that needed repairing, paint that was chipping and ground that was eroding. He knew that it was vital to tend to any damage early before the full brunt of nature could do irreparable harm.

We are blessed to have our very own personal caretaker. Someone who lovingly knows all about us, all of our strengths and all of our weaknesses, and who longs to keep us whole and strong and be a beacon for the world, and for our children. Sure, we can stand for a time without someone tending to us but after awhile the salt in our wounds start to chip away at our strength and soon we begin to crumble. That someone is God.

God longs to be your caretaker. He already knows you inside and out, and understands you better than you know yourself. God knew we were going to need help on this journey and that we were going to need His strength to handle some of the situations that we would encounter. God even wrote a book to tell us how to care for ourselves and to inform us on how much He loves us. It's called the Bible.

God's desire is to move into the inner core of our being and to not only assess our needs daily, but hourly and minute by minute and to be present in our lives. He wants a relationship with you that will guide and empower you on your journey. He wants to keep you from harm and allow you to stand tall as you confront the battering elements that will come your way.

The Bible is comprised of 66 individual books that basically tell us the same thing. "God created you, He loves you, He is sending you on a journey where He wants you to be able to navigate your way over the mountains and across the desert planes. He put you in this world as an imperfect being surrounded by other imperfect people. You were raised by imperfect parents and may have married an imperfect spouse and filled your home with a bunch of imperfect kids. He instructs us on how to deal with the flaws that surround us and He wants you to learn a few things on your journey but most importantly, He wants you to eventually come home and be with Him."

God knew the journey would be hard so He didn't send us without any help. He empowers us with His Holy Spirit that allows our light to shine even on the darkest days. The Holy Spirit is a powerful force that lives within us if we ask. His presence in our life allows us to "grow fruit" which are nine character traits that are ours for the asking. The scripture tells us that the Holy Spirit allows "fruit" to grow in us so that we may share our gifts with the world.

Galatians 5:22 tell us that the Fruit of the Spirit are: *Love, Joy, Peace, Patience, Kindness, Goodness, Faithfulness, Gentleness, and Self-control.* Wouldn't we all love to have some of that fruit especially a big dose of patience when we are in the middle of raising teenagers? How do you grow some of this fruit? You just ask for it. You pray to God to empower you with some joy or self-control. If your desire is there, the Holy Spirit will come. How do I know this? Because I lacked most of the fruit on the list when I was a young mom and I knew that what I was doing wasn't working. So I prayed and asked God for help and then became a student of His word. Today I am actually shocked at the patience that I have. It certainly didn't come from my own power but from the care of my personal Lighthouse keeper.

The Holy Spirit dwells inside us and allows our fruit to grow. His presence allows our light to shine. We begin to feel joy and then we can see our light shining brightly even on the darkest of days. We will feel God's peace, His love, and His joy even as the world is attacking us with a battering storm. The Bible reminds us over and over again that God longs to send you His peace. Isn't that a comforting thought when we are in the midst of a battle?

God knew that parenting wasn't going to be an easy job but it certainly is an important one, just as the lighthouse holds a vital role for those sailors out at sea. The sailors counted on the light to guide them home just as our kids are counting on us to be there to guide them to safety. The comfort that the beaconing light brings to the sailors who are encountering rough seas and the dangers of a jagged coastline is the same comfort that a child feels when they arrive safely to a loving home. We need to be that for our kids. They are fighting their own battles and many times they are on rough seas in a very small boat. They are being battered and tossed by waves we may not even see. A small wave can frighten an inexperienced sailor so it is vital that we train them well for the swells that may come. We need to help them maintain their balance so that as the waves build they will be ready for the turbulence. Many times the waves are so large that their tiny boat seems to be swallowed up as they go up and down with the surf. We can't see their little boat as they are in the trough of the rolling surf. It is frightening as we search for their little boat as it goes up and down in the waves. What we need to always remember is that we may not see them but they can see us, that tall beacon on the cliff! They need us to be strong and bright so that they don't lose heart. They may tremble, but they know that we are there looking out for them. Our light may be the only hope they see.

It is vital to keep your light bright but sometimes that is hard when we are being battered by life ourselves. The pressures of daily life can weigh you down and chip away at your very core. That is why it is important that we have an attentive lighthouse keeper who is tending to our needs.

Daily, the light keeper makes an inspection of the tower to be sure that it is a stable structure. If he sees some cracked and crumbling mortar he lovely chisels away the damage and points up the area by adding fresh mortar. Our tower may be scared by the repair but if it is done correctly it should sustain us and allow us to continue to do our job effectively.

That is how God treats us. He knows everything about us and when He sees an area that needs attention He will use His chisel and chip away at the damage. Sometimes it is painful but always it is necessary for it prevents more extensive damage down the road. God will tend to your needs so that you will have the ability to tend to the needs of others. If he sees an area that needs addressing he will make your life uncomfortable until you tend to the problem. He will rob you of your peace and cause you restless nights until you pay attention and repair the damage that that wound is causing.

In **John 16:33** we are told "I have said these things to you, that in me you may have **peace**. In this world you will have trouble. But take heart; I have overcome the world."

Whenever I feel that my peace is gone (and that can be frequent raising four children) I need to pause and assess my life and discover where or when I was robbed of my peace. Maybe I spoke disrespectfully to my husband, perhaps I shared a piece of gossip about a friend, or maybe I responded cruelly to my child when they sassed me. Whatever it is, I can usually discover it pretty quickly since I try to do a daily assessment of my state of being. I may sometimes experience a restless night but I rarely experience more then the loss of one restful night of sleep. My life is too busy to go too many nights without sleep so I put my concerns to prayer and usually it becomes very obvious where the damage is. Once I am aware of the problem I may need to have a painful chiseling away of the problem (apologize to the friend that I spoke ill of) or maybe it just needs a small bit of mortar (lovingly hug my kids and explain that I am sorry that mom lost her cool). Whatever the situation, the sooner I address it, the smaller the repair will be. I have learned that the longer I wait the bigger the damage and the harder the repair.

A lighthouse keeper is vital to the health of the tower and I can't imagine going through this journey without an attentive one. God assesses my needs daily and informs me when damage is noted.

If I feel lonely ... His words remind me that He is beside me.

If I feel unloved ... I am reminded that He calls me precious child, He created me and loves me.

If I feel anxious ... He tells me to be anxious for nothing, and to not be afraid but bring my concerns to Him with prayer and petition and He will give me peace.

If I lack joy ... He tells me that He sent His Spirit to live in me so that I may experience not only Joy but Love, Peace, Patience, Kindness, Goodness, Faith, Gentleness and Self-control in all situations.

I am so thankful that my lighthouse keeper looks out for me. That He daily makes sure that I am in good condition so that I may effectively do my job. Trust him to do the same for you and before long your light will be shining brightly even on the darkest days.

CHAPTER 3
The Light Shines
Even In The Bright Of Day

⟿

Have you ever noticed that the beacon of the lighthouse is always on. It shines during the dark of night, the blanket of fog, the raging storms, and even the brightness of the day. It is always there to provide its direction to a passing vessel.

The same is true with parenting; you need to always be on. Always ready to offer guidance, direction, and warnings. It is a 24/7 job and one where you can't afford to go dark, or to be missing.

Your child needs the reassurance that you are there every day, every hour, and every minute. They need to know that they can depend on you during both the calm days, and the raging storms. It's a tough and exhausting job.

It isn't easy to be there to listen to your daughter go into every detail about the movie she just saw when you have already put in eight hours at an exhausting job. It isn't easy to make it to their games at 5 p.m. when you would much rather go home and just chill. It isn't easy to be enjoying a night out at dinner and have to go home early because your child just threw up on the babysitter. When you become a parent you need to change from a life that is self-centered to one that is selfless. It's what I like to call "Being there!"

It means that you are not just present in your child's life but you are in their presence. That means being engaged with who they are, and what they do. It means knowing their friends, knowing what their concerns are, and paying attention to their strengths as well as their weaknesses. Taking the time to know them in the light of day and the dark of night.

Our church ran a youth ski retreat and I was involved with leading it for 20 years. There were times when we had more than 50 kids attending and believe me managing a group of 7th to 12th graders for a weekend wasn't always easy. One of the highlights of the event came on Saturday night after two days of skiing, many meals and our retreat lessons, we had an awards presentation. I brought along a box full of "junk" … small trinkets that I saved all year (Happy Meal toys, garage sale trinkets, etc). The chaperones put their heads together and came up with an award for each child. Not only did we have to pay attention to some 50 or so kids, but we had to look through my box of "junk" and find an award that went with the story. A pair of baby socks for the skier who had cold feet about going up the mountain, sparking rocks for two siblings that clashed, a comb for the boy with wild hair. Little stories about each child with a token of remembrance. It took a lot of work as we had to pay attention to each child and we had a short time to do it. We had to look at each person uniquely so that we could acknowledge them accordingly. The reward that we received for our effort was that each child felt valued. They felt like they mattered and someone cared about them. I was told years later that one boy still had the comb I gave him for his hair. The boy next to him told me that his trinket was still on his desk at home.

We took the time to pay attention to all of the kids on the retreat. We noticed who needed support on the mountain and who needed support on the social front. We encouraged our older students to be role models and look out for the younger participants, and made sure that everyone felt safe. It took a lot of energy but it was so worth it. Parenting requires that same commitment. It is exhausting to constantly pay attention to each of our kids but it is vital that you step up to the challenge. They notice and they will know if the TV or phone is more important than they are.

There was an article published recently that told the story of a boy in school who had to write an essay on the topic "My wish..." His response was very telling as he responded that he wished he could be a smartphone. "My parents like smartphones very much. They are so fond of it that they forget about me. My father comes home tired from the office and goes immediately to his phone. He has time to play games on it and not with me. When the phone rings my parents answer immediately but they don't bother with me even if I am crying. That's why I want to become a smartphone."

How tragic. Sadly, I am sure that there are children all over this country who feel the same way. I was at lunch one day and I saw a father completely immersed on his phone while his son sat across from him in his baseball uniform staring into space. My heart broke for that little boy and I wanted so badly to go over to the father and tell him that his little boy needed his attention and to put the phone away. Time flies by so quickly and this one-on-one time with your child will be gone in a moment.

Children know when they are valued and when they are dismissed. I challenge you to make a rule in your home that no phones are to be used at the dinner table and everyone must wait at least five minutes when they come in the door before they can look at a phone or computer screen. Pause for just a few minutes to acknowledge the most important people in your life, and the reward will be that each family member will feel valued.

Another aspect of parenting that is vital for your child to learn is to have a clear vision of where they are going. Life is a challenging journey but it can be even more challenging without a roadmap to guide you on your way. It's important for them to know how to navigate the twists and turns that they may encounter and to know what to do if they hit a roadblock. They need to have the tools to help them and to know what to do if conditions change.

I always felt that it was important for my kids to know what to do if an unexpected situation occurred. When they started kindergarten I gave each of them a key to the front door and hid it in one of the pockets of their backpack. I was always home when they got off the bus from school but if the unexpected occurred and perhaps I was stuck in traffic or got delayed at the grocery store I wanted them to have the tools to help themselves. I wanted them to know that they could go safely into the house and wait for me. We prepared them for an emergency. Since they knew they had a key they never needed to worry about coming home and not being able to get in the house. They felt safe. A neighbor's child once came to our home in the pouring rain because she was locked out of her home and her mom wasn't there. I never wanted my kids to feel as helpless as she did. To not have a safe place to go.

You can't anticipate every situation but by helping them know what to do in some situations it allows them to think through the problem and hopefully gain their own wisdom.

God gives us that same reassurance in the Gospel of John (John 14:2). He is preparing to leave them and doesn't want them to be anxious about not knowing the plan. He wants to reassure them that He is going ahead and preparing a place for them. We hear Jesus tell the Apostles "In my Father's house there are many rooms; if that were not so, would I have told you that? I am going there to prepare a place for you." When they didn't understand where He was going we have the most beautiful response to their concerns: "I am the way and the truth and the life. No one comes to the Father except through me." He told us how to get home and He told us that He would light the way.

How comforting to know that God is aware of our concerns, that He sent His Son to show us the way and that He even sent His Holy Spirit to guide us on our journey. He tells us over and over to not be anxious, and that He wants to bring us His peace. He wants a relationship with us that includes a key to the front door.

God is telling us that He wants to be our Father and He calls us to be His child. All we have to do is say YES! We are heirs to His throne and we will receive His promise that when this journey is over, we can safely arrive in Heaven and a room will be waiting for us.

When I teach this lesson to my Confirmation class I actually present them with a key on a lanyard. I let them know that God is preparing a room for them and He is asking them to be part of His family. All they have to do is say "Yes, I want to be a child of God." The promise that we receive when we make the choice to be in His family is that He will be with us on the journey and when the journey is complete we will have a room with our name waiting for us in heaven. We don't have to knock and hope the door opens, we can travel confidently knowing that the key will fit and it will let us in.

Make sure your children learn this lesson as it will allow them to walk confidently on this foreign soil knowing that a heavenly home awaits them. Remind them that they are heirs to the King and that they should conduct themselves as such. Walking with confidence that the God who overcame death is their Heavenly Father. Let them hide this valuable truth in their heart and they will see the world from a different perspective. They will have peace during storms, confidence during battles, and love during trials.

It is hard to teach this lesson if you have a hard time knowing this truth yourself. Do you know that God loves you? Do you know that He calls you to live with Him in a heavenly home? Do you know that He wants you to experience His fruit? If you don't feel God's presence in your life you can change that by simply asking for it. Realize though, that it may be hard to hear God's voice if your behavior is blocking the connection. If you treat others with disrespect, or if anger is overwhelming your relationships, you may have to put yourself in a calm place and call out to God for His help and wisdom. Rest assured that He hears you and he wants to have a relationship with you. Just keep calling home and reaching out to Him, before you know it you will start to see evidence of God working in your life.

What are some things that you can do to change the dynamics in your home and allow everyone to feel valued and respected? Pause and look at your family dynamics. Do you respond fairly to each of your children or do you play favorites? Do you engage everyone in the care of your home or do you act like a maid and a servant to the needs of your kids? Do you treat your spouse with respect and command that your children do the same? It is vital to assess the health of your home, especially when things are calm, so that when the trials of life come, your home's foundation is secure and you can all weather the storms successfully.

Sometimes it is the small gestures that you do during the light of day that will hold your child's heart during the dark of night. Being there during the relatively easy years of third grade will assure them that you will be there during the turbulent years of seventh grade. They see your presence in their lives and feel valued. You store in their hearts the knowledge that they are loved and cared for ... that they matter. They have an understanding that they are a valuable part of the family.

I like to encourage the fathers to really step up during the sixth through eighth grade years. You usually enter this chapter in relative calm seas but you may end this chapter in turbulent waters. If a father isn't present, perhaps an uncle or a grandfather can take an active role in their lives. You want to cultivate a relationship while the seas are calm so that you lay the foundation for what challenges may be ahead. Perhaps plan a date night that involves just dad and child, a night just one on one with them for dinner, or to a sporting event. Some private time that sets the stage for those same outings when the drama is more intense. Little things that the child can count on. A Valentine's dinner on the Saturday before February 14th for a father and daughter. Supper at the diner and a local football game for the father and son. Whatever activity that you both like that will set the stage for some quality time when they really need it. My father took me golfing and I cherish those outings and even wrote a book about it: "Lessons I Learned From My Father While Playing Golf" that I gave him for his 80th birthday. It was a book that told him that I paid attention to the little details that he taught me while we hit a ball around a course. Things like: don't take yourself too seriously; you get 18 chances to start over; and maintain the flow of the game. Lessons that I not only learned on the golf course but lessons that I applied to my life. Not that moms can't have a special outing with their children but up to this point I find that moms do much of the heavy lifting in their child's early years and now it is time for the dads to build those bonds that the child needs.

It is also important to cultivate family chores, so children can learn how to help with the management of the home. This not only gives them life skills but it teaches them that they are an important part of the family. Your job as a parent is to help your child be an independent, self-sufficient, responsible adult. It takes time to achieve this goal and you can't accomplish that the week before they go away to college. When you look at the big picture and realize that the main goal is to teach them to take responsibility for themselves it will begin to direct your actions. The point is that you want to take advantage of the calm moments in your family's life to spend some time teaching. Life goes by very quickly and if you don't develop a plan of action for instruction you may find yourself with a teenager who is clueless about managing their life, both physically and emotionally.

The lesson for us parents to understand is that our job is to model and teach our children what it means to be a responsible adult. To help them to understand that actions have consequences and that they are part of this family and with that comes expectations that they need to contribute to the well being of the whole family. Cultivating a team effort requires time and patience but as any successful coach knows the rewards of success are greatly increased when everyone does their part.

Your number one job will be to keep your light shining brightly whether it's a sunny day or you are experiencing the darkness of a moonless night. How do you generate enough energy to keep that light shining for the long haul? You pray.

Prayer helps you bond with God, bond with your children and help your kids bond with you. It is calling on a power greater than yourself to watch over your family. When your children know that you are praying for them, they feel protected and loved by you. As you pray, one of the first things that you need to ask God for is to heal any wounds that you may have. Things in your life that rob you of your peace and prevent you from modeling that peace to your children.

As we pray for ourselves we need to ask God how we can be the best parent possible for our children. There is something about prayer that fills us with wisdom and confidence and reassures us that we aren't on this journey alone. By utilizing prayer we can ask God to strengthen us with the "Ten P's":

1. Purpose ... Helping me to point my children in the right direction.
2. Peace ... Helping me to stay calm when my children frustrate me.
3. Perspective ... Help me to see things from God's perspective.
4. Protectiveness ... Guarding them from things I can't protect them from.
5. Positive words ... Help me to use words that are positive and encouraging.
6. Passion ... Help me to be committed to God, my partner, and my children.
7. Patience ... Letting things happen in God's timing.
8. Provision ... Help me to be attentive to their basic needs.
9. Purity ... Help me to model the right words, actions and attitudes.
10. Perseverance ... Help me to show love over the long haul.

Once I pray for myself, then I need to pray over my children. I ask God to keep them healthy and safe. I ask Him to help them to make wise choices. I pray that immaturity, inexperience, peer pressures, and negative influences won't leave a permanent scar. I pray that temptations won't lead them astray and that they develop strength of character. I also pray for their friends and future spouse. I ask God to help my children develop a relationship with Him as their Father and allow them to be comforted by His presence.

Cultivating a home of faith requires time and effort. **Joshua 24:15** "As for me and my household, we will serve the Lord." It takes time to till the soil of our children's faith. It takes time to attend worship, pray in the evening, and get your children to Sunday school. But it is time well spent as you are building their foundation and giving them tools to use throughout their entire life. Nothing that you give your child is more valuable.

So how do you start building and cultivating your child's faith? You till their soil and allow the seeds of faith to take root. The seeds are good and your job as a parent is to loosen the soil so that it is able to receive those seeds. Begin by praying for them. Prayer works. Kids know this. When they are scared, they want you to pray. When somebody is hurt, they want you to pray. When they are ready for bed, they want you to pray.

In a world of dangers, temptations, and challenges, your children desperately need your prayers. This may be the most important thing you do all day. (More important than paperwork, lunch meetings, golf, laundry, or yard work.) Your children are your gift from God and you need to treat them as such. You are their stewards and you need divine guidance to help you mentor them properly.

Ask God to fill you with His wisdom. Seek His guidance and pause long enough to hear His voice. As you become a wisdom seeker you can start to see His hand in your life, and the lives of your family members. By pausing to be in God's presence, you are able to tune out the chaos around you and gain His wisdom. Find time to be quiet and turn off the noise of the world, and when you do you may start to hear God's voice. I wrote these words in the front of my Bible as a reminder to do just that, "Make time for quiet moments, as God whispers and the world is loud."

If we don't take time to separate from the grind of this world and pause to spend some quality time with our Heavenly Father, then our children won't know the value of doing the same. We need to seek a sure footing so that when the storms come we are able to stand against the elements. That occurs when we cultivate a relationship with our God that will sustain us on our journey. As we gain knowledge about His promises, then we begin to grow in wisdom. He made many promises to us, but one of His greatest promise is that He will grant us peace. As you cultivate your relationship with your Heavenly Father you will start to feel that peace, and then you will begin to see His presence modeled in your life. Do you feel that peace? Do your children? How about your spouse?

Take baby steps to begin this journey if you don't feel God's presence. Relationships require time and attention. Think of reading the Bible as time spent reading a letter from a loved one. Begin with reading Psalms or Proverbs and just meditate on a verse or two at a time. Let the message sink in and marinate during your day. Share it with your family at dinner, and ask them what they think of the scripture. Listen to Christian music, and let that set the tone on your drive to work or dropping the kids off at school. Attend worship, and focus on being in God's presence verses just being present in the building. Listen to how many times the word "peace" is used, and let that comfort you.

These are all ways to bring God closer to your family. If we never mention His name then pretty soon we forget that He is there. Let His name be heard frequently in your home, and then your children will think of Him as an important family member.

I used to send my youngest son off to school with these words, "Have a good, and Godly day." Maybe that is a motto that you want to adopt as you send your child out the door.

CHAPTER 4
Calm Seas

~·~

C hange. That is the one thing that is true about sailing, you are always experiencing changes. The weather is always changing and sailing is a sport that is entirely dependent on the weather. One day you might have a breeze from the South that is calm and steady and the next day the wind is from the North with cooler and puffier breezes. You need to adjust daily for the changes in the weather not only in what you wear but also how you trim your sails. It is important to understand your boat and know how it responds to choppy waters or puffy winds. You need to learn how to make it go at its optimum speed when the breeze is light and how to gybe without capsizing when the winds are blowing. The goal is to become a student of both yourself and your boat.

That is also true of our life journey. Our world changes daily and we need to adjust to those changes if we want to have a successful voyage. When we become parents we change from the role as a child ourselves to that of being the caregiver of a child. The grandparents move up the ladder and they go from being a parent to a role with less responsibility and input. Sometimes we can navigate these changes with little disruption and other times there is major conflict as the roles in the family changes. Grandparents fail to relinquish the role of primary caregiver and want to continue to be in charge. That may cause major conflict as there becomes a battle over control. The goal is to understand the changing roles and to learn to communicate effectively. Now add the addition of a child and their unique personality and you have another area of change. I see all too often that parents fail to realize that their child is always growing and developing. What worked for them at one stage may not work at another. Just as the sea and weather are in a constant state of change so is your family home and the world around you.

As a parent it is important to help our children know who they are and what gifts they were given so that they will learn how to navigate the daily changes. The time to learn these things isn't in the storms of life but in the calm seas where the lesson can be taught and mastered before the storms hit. This is especially hard to teach when the parent themselves don't have a clue of what their strengths are or where they are headed. This is a chapter that will address the issue about learning and peace. How to become a student of oneself and to experience the peace that comes from accepting yourself just as you were made.

Some boats were built for speed, others for stability. Some were built to transport and others to race. It's important to know what kind of boat you were given and what type of boat your child is steering. The Bible tells us that each of us are given gifts by God that will empower us during our lifetime. God promised each of us at least one gift and the more we cultivate the gifts that we were given the more He may entrust us with.

When I was in junior high I was painfully shy. If you spoke to me I would turn a bright shade of red and I could feel heat radiating up my face, which only added to my humiliation. I barely looked up when someone asked me a question and I would never volunteer for something that put me in the spotlight. I realized that I had a problem and something inside me told myself that I needed to change or I wouldn't be useful for what God wanted me to do.

It wasn't easy but when I was a freshman in high school I signed up for a public speaking class. I wasn't sure what that really meant but it sounded like something I needed. Little did I realize that at the end of the semester I would be speaking in front of the entire school during an assembly. As a freshman I had to speak in front of the seniors so you can imagine what I was feeling. I was nervous, but you know what? I did it! I realized that it wasn't as bad as I imagined and little did I know that my career would eventually find me speaking in front of an auditorium full of people when I teach the Maternity Orientation at my Medical Center. That one step influenced my life in so many ways and I see where God has empowered me to do things that I would never have imagined in junior high school.

The challenge for all of us is to do our self discovery in the calm moments of our life, when the seas are smooth and the winds are steady and light. It is then that we have the time and clarity to see what gifts God empowered us with.

It is in these moments of peace that you can discover who you are , what are your strengths and in what areas of your life you may need improvement. If you know that you lack balance (a worka-holic), then take some moments to introduce elements of play into your life. Develop a hobby such as golf or bike riding to balance the drive that you may feel in the work field. If you find that your home is full of chaos then discover ways to bring order into your home. Having a plan for the day that is manageable, buying storage bins for items, cleaning out a drawer or closet each week, assigning tasks to each family member, are just some ways that you can bring order into your home. If your home is filled with disrespect, begin today to have a family meeting to bring honor and respect back into your home. If you lack peace or self-control, then today pray for these Fruits of the Spirit (Gal 5:22) and seek out ways to grow these fruits in your life. Whatever area of your life seems out of kilter it is during the calm seas that you should address it. Likewise, this is a time to nurture your strengths. What are your gifts, your strengths, and your passions? What brings you joy? It is in the calm waters of your life that you can strengthen these gifts and make sure that you are using them to their full potential. It is also during this time of calm that it is important to hide God's word in your heart. To take time to get to know who He is and what His promises are so that when the storms of life hit you have your Lifesaver close at hand. Dedicate time to find a church that feeds your family. Take time to open your Bible and become a student of His teachings and then share His words with your loved ones. Listen to Christian music so that it feeds your soul while you are doing your housework or driving to work. Memorize Bible verses that speak to you so that during the storms of your life, you can call out to God as you remember His promises.

Jeremiah 17:7-8
Blessed is the man who trusts in the Lord, whose hope is in Him. For he shall be like a tree planted by the waters, who spreads its roots by the river. He will not fear when the heat comes for its leaves will be green and he will not be anxious in the year of the drought for he will bear fruit.

Isn't it wonderful when you get to experience the joy of calm seas and drift aimlessly along looking for the light breezes that will push you forward. This is the time in your life when you feel confident and good about yourself. When you are in sync with your spouse, your boss, and your kids. Everyone seems to be on the right track and slowly and steadily making forward progress. Life is Good!

Don't we wish that the entire journey would stay this way? Easy days with sunny skies and warm temperatures. But just like the heat stirs the atmosphere to create wind and fronts will push a nice high pressure system along and allow a low pressure system to take its place, replacing nice sunny days with stormy clouds... Changes they are a coming!!!

With that in mind if you happen to be in this nice high pressure system in your home take advantage of it before the weather changes. It may not necessarily be a storm but changes are constantly happening and our roles are always changing. Toddlers eventually become teenagers and one day those teenagers become adults and begin life on their own. As parents we go from caretakers for our children to possibly caretakers for our parents. We need to constantly adjust to these changes and to not only prepare ourselves but also our children for the changes that will come.

It is best to do these preparations while the seas are calm and you can instruct and advise while you aren't battling a storm. One of the first things to address is to help your child understand is who they are. That is a big and challenging task.

At the medical center where I work, I am involved with the education of new parents. I teach the newborn classes to the parents who are about to deliver their firstborn child. You can imagine that the anxiety level is high as they are clueless about what to expect. My goal is to instill confidence and reduce their anxiety level. Besides educating them on what a newborn will look and act like, I spend time talking to the them about the importance of becoming a student of their baby. Who are they? Who did they just give birth to? Do they like to guzzle their food or are they a nibbler? Do they love to sleep or is it a struggle to get them to nap? Each child is unique and as much as we would love to have a one size fits all approach, children come in all shapes, temperaments, and sizes (even within our own families) and our job is to discover who they are.

Your job as parents is to figure out who you just brought into the world. What are they like? What things calms them and what makes them upset? What do they like to eat, how do they like to sleep, are they content to play by themselves or do they constantly need to be entertained? I hate to tell you this but this job never ends. As long as you are a parent you will be studying your child to help them navigate this world. You will need to help them know what their strengths are and in what areas they show weakness. You will constantly be looking for teachable moments and opportunities that you can use to help them develop strengths where a weakness is evident like I did with my public speaking.

As a new parent we are always attentive to the dangers that surround our children. We teach them to not touch a hot stove, not run into the road, and not climb on things that can fall over. We are forever worried about their safety. If we could we would love to keep them in bubble wrap and protected from harm, but you can't always keep your children safe. Yet you can help teach them to be strong. That made me realize that my job wasn't to always protect them from danger, but to empower them to be strong and wise and understand the dangers around them.

As much as I would have loved to protect my children and keep them safe (safe from harm, bullies, disappointments, etc.) I knew that some of those trials are the very things that they may need to strengthen them later. It was vital that I spend time in the early years (calm seas) teaching them how to navigate their boat so when the day comes that they will leave the safety of the harbor they have acquired the skills needed to navigate the open seas. I needed to teach them how to be strong so they would have the knowledge to steer their own ship. I wanted to help them have the ability to call on their own wisdom when confronted with the challenges that will face them each and every day. That begins with baby steps and the understanding that my job wasn't to do for them the things that they could do for themselves. To change from the role of being their caregiver to teaching them to care for themselves. To help them to learn how to handle their emotions and respond to challenges with wisdom. To learn the valuable gift of discernment and the ability to make wise choices. To cultivate a sense of confidence in them to think for themselves, choose friends wisely, and see the big picture for their lives. A great challenge indeed!

Before we can successfully guide our children it helps if we first know ourselves. Many parents don't fully understand their own gifts and strengths so it can make it hard to help our kids understand theirs. It is a challenge to study yourself and discover what your passions are and what you are destined to do with this life of yours. By being a student of yourself you begin to see what strengths you have and how you can use those strengths to navigate your own journey. As you learn to understand yourself, then you will gain the tools to help your child discover who they are and then you can be that tall lighthouse on the hill guiding and lighting their path.

Life is a journey of learning. I found that I was always looking for opportunities to instruct. If we went to the grocery store, I would have them look for the fruit we needed. They could weigh it and then determine about how much it would cost. If my husband was building something he liked to have the kids help so that they gained some knowledge about basic tools. We encouraged them to cook some meals and involved them in planning our vacations. We looked for opportunities to educate our children anywhere we could find them.

The one thing that I learned being the mother of four was that each one of them had a different personality, and I realized early that I needed to approach each child from a perspective that fit their personality. My daughter was responsible and organized where my one son was fun loving and a procrastinator. Homework was a joy for my daughter and something to be dreaded from my son. I needed to discover who they were so that I could best parent them.

There are wonderful resources on the market that can help you gain wisdom about personality types. They provide insight that can help you identify not only who you are but also what type of personality your child has. When you gain knowledge about personality types it helps you gain wisdom about why you may be experiencing a conflict with one child and not another. It may help you understand why one child is content with one true friend and another child has the need to have lots of friends. By gaining wisdom you will be able to guide them on their career path and understand that the outgoing child may thrive in sales but would be bored to death in accounting. Another influence on your child's personality may be their birth order. The oldest child tends to be a high achiever while the youngest child may reach outside the home for affirmation. These are generalizations but it is interesting to see how your family dynamics work.

I have a friend who is taking care of her mother with the help of her siblings. Each sibling has a different strength and so they were able to tap into what each one is good at. One sibling took care of the finances, another drove her to the doctor appointments. One helps with her daily care and another prepares meals for the week. Each was able to tap into their strengths and the burden was lightened. They understood that the sibling who was good at math and delighted in management issues was not good with the gentle spirit needed to be a caregiver. It allowed each to use their strengths for the best outcome.

While the seas are calm it is a good time to explore your family dynamics and get a good grasp of what each person brings to the table. This is also a wonderful time to establish family traditions. These traditions can come in every size and shape. Some are fancy while others are simple. Some require money and others are free. Yet every tradition, no matter how big or small , makes a powerful impact. Kids like patterns. In a world that sometimes feel chaotic and out of control, traditions provide a sense of order and security. They give us something to hold on to. When children are faced with stress or trauma, they cling to the familiar. They want to know what to expect and what is predictable so they can relax and feel safe. Traditions are all those activities and events that make your family unique. They build memories and bring us joy along with helping us bond with the members of our family. Traditions don't just happen by themselves but they require some effort and planning. What traditions do you remember as a child? What traditions are you establishing in your home? Begin today to establish some traditions that your children will one day cherish.

While the atmosphere is calm you can help a child feel valuable by spending some quality time with them. Today's kids have a tougher journey than any other generation in terms of social pressures. Facebook and social media can rob a child's sense of self worth and value very quickly and can leave them vulnerable. Parents often feel helpless to equip their kids with the tools to navigate and steer clear of harmful relationships, behaviors, and attitudes that surround them. Just as the lighthouse stands guard and looks for trouble we also need to be on constant guard for the dangers that our children may encounter. By helping them develop strengths and letting them experience consequences for their actions we help them to grow and learn from their mistakes.

The process of equipping our kids to not only live but to thrive in the world begins as soon as they are born. Parents are the single most important influence in a child's life.

If you bungle raising your children, I don't think whatever else you do matters very much. Jackie Kennedy

I don't care how old your child is, it is never too late to build a relationship with them. In the Bible we have a story of encouragement titled the Prodigal Son. (Luke 15:11-32) It is the story of two sons who work on their father's estate. One of the son decides that he wants to get his share of his inheritance and leave home. The father is heartbroken but obliges. The son wastes his inheritance money on a sinful lifestyle of drinking and partying. He has lots of friends and lives the good life... until his money runs out. His friends desert him and he is reduced to cleaning the pig sties. He realizes that his father's servants live better than he does so he decides to return home and tell his father that he has sinned against God and him and that he would like to return and be a servant in his father's house.

Little does he know that his father hasn't forgotten him. His father has been patiently waiting for him to return. You can only imagine how wounded the father's heart is as he worries about how his son is doing and if he is okay. As the son turns up the drive to his former home he wonders what the reception will be. The beauty of the story is that the father is watching for him. He is looking down the drive hoping that one day his son will return to the safety of the nest. No condemnation, no "I told you so," no anger, only hope. When the father sees the son there is pure joy as he runs to greet his wayward child. There isn't even a chance to repent for the father has called for a banquet and a killing of the fatted calf. There is to be a celebration that the child who was lost has been found. The other sibling is angry that he was the loyal son and there is no celebration for him. The father lovingly explains to him "Son, you are always with me, and all I have is yours. It was right that we should make merry and be glad, for your brother was dead and is alive again, he was lost and now is found."

The father's response is the same as God's response is to us. He showed forgiveness, acceptance, rejoicing, grace and unconditional love. Center your relationship with your child on commitment, perseverance, grace and lots of prayer. Help them to feel good about themselves and an acceptance of who they are.

When you assist your child in helping them forge a strong, positive identity they will learn to like themselves and understand their strengths and weaknesses and that will allow them to stand firm regardless of what is happening around them. They will know which side of the fence they belong and be able to boldly proclaim who they are. The Bible tells us that we are either wise or foolish and our goal as parents is to help them choose wisdom.

How do you build a child who can stand tall in the face of adversity, who shows compassion and kindness and makes wise decisions? Step by step.

A mason approaches building a rock wall by first doing an intense study of the material that he has to use. Some rocks are round, some are flat and some are just plain odd. They differ in color and texture. A mason must study the design to see how these rocks will fit into the final plan. Remember a mason will use what he is given and that will determine the outcome. He studies his material and lays out the rocks so that he has knowledge about how they will fit together. How well do you know your material? The job of building a wall is messy and requires hands-on application and commitment. Sounds a lot like parenting. Parents need to labor beside them to help them decide which rocks fit and which one's don't. They need to see the value of the material they are given and use that material to make their own unique wall. The challenge is to make them who *God* made them to be rather than who *we* want them to be. Maybe the greater challenge is for us to learn that lesson as parents.

How can we make a difference in our children's life? Brick by brick.

BRICK #1
ENCOURAGE SELF-DISCOVERY

When was the last time that you truly studied the person that you were given to care for? Do you know their strengths and what gifts they have? Are they similar to you or your spouse or totally different? Do they understand what their gifts are? The challenge is to help them understand themselves and be willing to be the unique person that God made them to be. If you don't cultivate a sense of self-discovery, your child will be like a chameleon that will blend into whatever situation they are in or change with whoever they are with. Help them to learn the phrase "To thine own self be true."

BRICK #2
ACKNOWLEDGE NATURAL ABILITIES

Children yearn for our support and they long to have a relationship with us. It's important to affirm their natural abilities (even if they are different from ours) and celebrate the unique person they are. Be their cheerleader! Attend activities, even if they say "It's no big deal." Everyone needs to feel like they matter. Yes, it takes time and effort and yes, sitting on the couch mindlessly in front of the TV may seem more appealing than being on a cold bleacher, but believe me the rewards that you will gain will be worth every minute. Strive to be supportive and encouraging and try to remember that it's not about you. You had your turn, this is their journey.

Encourage them to stay involved, especially in high school when the pressures become greater. Challenge the artistic student to try a new instrument, audition for a play, take a watercolor class, or voice lessons. If they like to argue, consider the debate team. Talk about career choices that use their talents. If the high school sports team is too much pressure for them, consider finding a recreational team or encourage them to find a new sport to get involved in. Help them to tap into their strengths so that when the time comes for college or a trade school they are already on a path to their career choice. Help them see where they fit in, and look for opportunities for them to make new friends so they don't put all of their eggs in one basket. Encourage them to discover what they like and help them not to be overly influenced by their friends. Empower them to be bold enough to know what speaks to them and help them to try not to take themselves too seriously either. Lastly, reaffirm that they shouldn't be afraid of failure. Some of the greatest success stories came out of failures. Just read the life story of Thomas Edison or Michael Jordan. As we become adults we tend to develop a fear of failure. We are so afraid to try something because we might fail but when we think about children they live their life surrounded by failed attempts. Little babies fall a lot, yet they continue to try until they learn how to walk. Young boys and girls learn to ride a bike by failing at balance, but eventually they learn how to control the bike and the world is opened up to them. They fail all the time, but they don't think of themselves as failures. As we age we start to worry about failures and that holds us back. When something goes wrong, use it as a teaching moment with your child and help them learn from it. They will make mistakes, so the first time an infraction occurs make it a teachable moment and outline why what they did was wrong. If it occurs a second time then educate them that there will be consequences. The goal is to learn wisdom.

If you help your child cultivate their natural ability, they know who they are and they are excited about what their future has to offer.

BRICK #3
CREATE A FAMILY MOTTO

"As for me and my house, we will serve the Lord."

If you asked your kids what your family motto is could they tell you? Do they know what the rules are, what are the family goals, and what is your family's story? Is there a sense of pride in your family? I am going to tell you something that may be painful. Pride in your family starts with you. The parents set the tone for the home and without a clear direction the family can flounder. I think nothing is more important than the idea that in our family we treat each other with **honor and respect.** Begin today to draw a magna carta for your family. An understanding of who we are, what we believe in, and where are we going? Develop a motto for your home. It could be simple like "The Smiths aren't quitters" to something spiritual, but by establishing a family motto it gives your home a sense of identity. "In our home we don't speak like that" sends a message about what is expected not only as an individual but as a family unit. When difficulties arise, your motto serves as a stake in the ground declaring who you are and what you stand for as a family. It gives a sense of identity.

BRICK #4
VALUE DOWN TIME

Physically and emotionally, children live in a world of constant change. They can feel over scheduled, unknown, abandoned, or even betrayed. They see the world through a narrow lens and they feel threatened by the smallest disruption such as a friend inviting someone else over to their home and not your child. They need to have a safe place where they can let these changing emotions out and where they feel safe. They need to know that they belong and that their presence matters.

Make a point to welcome your family members when they come home. Take a pause from whatever you are doing and greet your spouse and children when they come in the door. Be sure to have the porch light on if family members will be coming home after dark. Nothing is sadder than coming home to a dark house after along day on the battlefield. Be sure that your home allows the family members to sigh with relief and a sense of peace when they walk through the door that they are now safe and secure. It doesn't take more that a few minutes but what you will gain will be priceless.

Let them know that you miss them when they are away from home and that they are an important part of the family dynamics. Help them see themselves as valuable by valuing them.

Encourage your child to enjoy down time, which strengthens their creativity and problem solving skills. Help them to be comfortable with some time to just daydream and ponder. We live in such a busy world so it is important to pull away sometimes and allow great things to happen as their minds get a chance to rest and explore.

BRICK #5
HIGHLIGHT SPIRITUAL GIFTS

Help your child know and understand what their Spiritual gifts are. God tells us that we are all given at least one of the Spiritual gifts and many of us have more than one.

In **Romans 12:3-8** Paul informs us of the different gifts:

For by the grace given me I say to every one of you: Do not think of yourself more highly than you ought, but rather think of yourself with sober judgment, in accordance with the faith God has distributed to each of you. For just as each of us has one body with many members, and these members do not all have the same function, so in Christ we, though many, form one body, and each member belongs to all the others. We have different gifts, according to the grace given to each of us. If your gift is prophesying, then prophesy in accordance with your faith; if it is serving, then serve; if it is teaching, then teach; if it is to encourage, then give encouragement; if it is giving, then give generously; if it is to lead, do it diligently; if it is to show mercy, do it cheerfully.

You can also read about Spiritual gifts in **1 Cor. 12:1-31**

If you see that your child has a gift for teaching then look for ways to expose them to teaching opportunities, maybe by helping a younger sibling with homework. If you see the gift of serving demonstrated in your child look for ways for your child to serve by perhaps helping in a soup kitchen or volunteering at a hospital. If they display leadership qualities be sure that they lead with kindness and encouragement. Always be on guard to see what gifts your child demonstrates and don't forget to become a student of yourself and what your gifts are as well.

BRICK #6
REINFORCE SPIRITUAL IDENTITY

No brick is more foundational than this one. When your child understands their value to God they can reject negative thinking that peers, insecurities, and problems hurl on them. Just because they fail, and we all fail, doesn't mean that they think of themselves as failures. Children (and adults) develop confidence when they believe they are loved by God ... no matter what. This inner strength will carry them through trials and peer pressure. As they search for significance they will find that they know how to stand firm when the ground around them is shaking. They will be able to hold themselves to a higher standard because they are heirs to a King and they know what is expected of them. They hold themselves in check when no one is looking because they know that their Heavenly Father is holding them accountable. They are able to lead others because they clearly know where the path is. They are on the road to heaven and they don't want to make a detour.

Building your child's identity is a long process. The Great Wall of China took years of extensive labor before it was able to fend off enemies. Our children live in a hostile culture too. They need protection. As parental masons, we can help them build a wall that will stand the test of time. It will protect them during trials and keep their enemies at bay. It will be a wall of character that is admirable by all who see it.

They are children of the King and so are you. Don't forget it!!!

CHAPTER 5

Lifesavers

~·~

I am a competitive sailor and I have been since I was 16 years old. Sailing is an exciting sport but one in which you are totally dependent on the weather. If there isn't any wind you spend your time on the shore socializing with your competitors. If it is too windy, you sit on shore socializing with your competitors, and if there is a thunder storm, likewise you sit on shore. But otherwise, you are on the water working together with your team to compete against the other racers. You need to be constantly aware of the changing conditions on the water and the always changing direction of the wind. If the wind is light you are searching for that light breeze that will surge you forward. If the wind conditions are strong you are looking for that calm moment when you can safely jibe without fear of a capsize. It is a sport where you need to be attentive to the ever-changing conditions around you. It is not much different in parenting.

The conditions are constantly changing and you need to adjust your sails to properly meet those changing winds. Likewise as a parent you need to be constantly aware of the changing conditions in your home and influences outside of you home that will impact the success of your family. It is vital to be aware of changing tides, shifting winds and impending storms.

One of the most important pieces of equipment that a sailor carries is a lifejacket for every team member. As conditions on the water change, the winds can quickly turn from a mild breeze to a dangerous squall in a matter of minutes. It is vital that everyone has a lifejacket when you see that the conditions are going downhill. In our Confirmation program at church one of the first lessons that I teach is about the importance of a lifesaver in their life. A lifesaver is vital to the sailor as it may be the one thing that will save them if disaster strikes. Likewise, having God as your lifesaver may save your family from impending disaster.

When you compete in a sailboat race it is mandatory that your boat carries enough lifejackets for everyone onboard. You don't always have to wear it during the race but if you finish the competition without a lifejacket onboard you can be disqualified. As any sailor knows a calm day on the water can quickly become deadly when you see a squall on the horizon. Being prepared is vital. If we see a storm coming the first thing we do is put on our lifejackets. If that storm hits and we capsize a lifejacket may be the only thing that will keep us afloat.

Another situation where I always wear a lifejacket is when I sail with lots of burdens such as four weather gear, or sailing boots. I want to be sure that I have my lifejacket on for if I get knocked overboard the burdens of all that gear can quickly pull me under the water. I need my lifejacket on to keep me afloat when all of my strength isn't enough to overcome the burdens that are trying to pull me under.

Life is like that. Storms can pop up in a moments notice or burdens that you don't even realize that you are carrying can pull you under and overwhelm you before you can call out for help.

I want my kids to know that they have a lifesaver who will be with them during the storms of their life or when burdens begin to overwhelm them. That lifesaver is God. All they have to do is make sure that they don't leave the shore without Him in their boat. I am known for always carrying "Lifesavers" as a reminder to them that God is their lifesaver. He will wrap His loving arms around them and keep them afloat when they can't rely on their own strength. When the storms of life hit them, they can face the impending uncertainty with the confidence that they are not alone. Someone who is greater than the storm is in the boat with them. He can calm the seas!

It is vital to empower your children with that knowledge. To remind them daily to not leave home without their lifesaver. Life is tough whether you are going to school, working at a full time job or managing a home. Storms can pop up in a moments notice. It is not a matter of "if" the storm comes but "when" the storm hits. It is important to give your child the tools they will need to manage the storm as best they can.

It is important to be prepared. When we see a squall on the horizon we immediately put on our lifejackets and then prepare for what may come. The lifejacket is first and foremost. Next we take a compass reading to make sure that we know what direction will lead us home. The storm may obscure our sight of the shoreline but our compass will keep us on the right heading to get to the safety of the harbor. Now it is time to readjust our sails. We may need to lower our mainsail, the largest sail, as the winds may be so powerful that they can capsize our boat if we are carrying too much sail. We rely on our smaller sail, the jib, to keep us going forward and make sure that we don't lose our ability to steer. Nothing is worse than having no power and being swept up in the movement of the water with no control over our direction. Our anchor and anchor line is readied so it may be cast overboard if the need is there to hold us in place if we need to guard against being pushed against a rocky shoreline. An anchor is the last resort to keep us from disaster. Now we are prepare to be battered by the storm.

As a parent it is important to prepare your child for those storms that may hit them. Make sure they have their lifejacket with them. A relationship with a Savior who will be beside them no matter what comes their way. You can't wait until the storm hits to go searching for your lifejacket. It must be with you and your child daily. It must be ready at a moment's notice. It must fit properly. That means that a Savior for a child is different from a Savior for a teenager. Let their relationship grow with the child. As they enter middle school it is important to bring a more durable and life sustaining jacket that will fit the increased weight of the child. Baby problems require one jacket but heavier problems require a more encompassing jacket to keep them afloat. Make sure you grow with your child so that you are aware of the need for a larger God to sustain them.

The Bible gives us a great example of how faith grows step by step and how to learn to trust God. In **Matthew 8:23-26** we get a clear example of what can happen when we have God in our boat.

Jesus Calms the Storm

23 Then he got into the boat and his disciples followed him. 24 Suddenly a furious storm came up on the lake, so that the waves swept over the boat. But Jesus was sleeping. 25 The disciples went and woke him, saying, "Lord, save us! We're going to drown!"
26 He replied, "You of little faith, why are you so afraid?" Then he got up and rebuked the winds and the waves, and it was completely calm.

What does this passage mean for us? First, it should remind you that even when you think God isn't there He tells us that He is right beside you waiting for you to call out to Him. Second, Jesus calmed the seas even though they had *little faith*. He doesn't require a deep level of faith to answer your call. Calling out is a simple sign of faith. When we cry out "Lord, help me!" no matter what the danger we are facing it is a prayer or plea that can calm the fiercest of storms. Anytime you turn to Him in prayer it is an act of faith. Lastly, the more you call out to God and see His faithfulness in calming your fears the more it builds confidence in your relationship with Him. We will always struggle with fears and concerns in this life because the world isn't a safe place. It is not our home, we are just travelers trying to make our way home to heaven. Just like the Apostles needed time to understand and trust who this Jesus was, so will we have to have patience to let our relationship with God grow. Building faith is a process but the comforting thing is that even in our fears and trials we may call out with our weak faith and say to Him, "Lord, help me!" Rest assured, He will awake and calm the seas.

Remember who is in the boat with you and take comfort in the fact that even the Apostles, experienced fishermen, were frighten by the storm. Eventually, they would face the storm head on and even sacrifice their lives for their Savior. But first they needed to learn to trust and that occurred lesson after lesson. Don't beat yourself up, just put on your lifejacket, cry out, and then just float as you watch what God can do in your life.

On our life journey we will also encounter burdens that threaten to pull us under. Things that weigh us down and cause us to be frightened. In sailing, it is vital for me to wear a lifejacket when the burdens I carry would pull me under if I fell out of the boat. The burdens of extra clothing or foul weather gear can quickly be an anchor that will pull me under the water if I didn't have a life jacket on to keep me afloat.

Life is like that. Too many times we leave the safety of our homes already weighed down with burdens before we close the front door. Then the smallest things can quickly cause us to capsize and now we are struggling to keep our heads above water. A simple trial soon becomes a major incident because we can't keep ahead of what is going on. Pretty soon we are literally fighting for our life.

If we have others in the mix with us, such as our spouse and children, soon we are pulling them under as we grasp for anything or anyone that will keep us afloat. We are in a panic and will lash out and attack anything that will help us survive. In a desire to keep our head above water we cling on to the nearest person and in the process we pull them under the water. Pretty soon we are all in a crisis and in danger of drowning. We are in a panic. It is at times like this when nothing is more comforting than having someone throw you a lifesaver as you feel like you are taking your last breath.

How do you save yourself and your family as well? You begin today to always remember to have your lifejacket with you. Pretty soon it is just habit. When I ran the junior sailing program at our sailing club the kids learned that as soon as class started until it ended they were to always be wearing their lifejacket. Maybe the first day or two they needed to be reminded but certainly after eight weeks they couldn't imagine not having it on. It became habit. Make talking to God a daily habit. Before you know it you can't imagine starting your day any other way. When I know my day is going to be especially busy that is when I know that I need to check in with God even more. I used to think sometimes that I was too busy to have prayer time; now I know that that is when I especially need that connection.

Life can get so busy and we can feel like there isn't time to connect with our creator but the Bible tells us over and over about the importance of connecting with God and resting with Him. In the beginning as He was creating the world God needed to rest from His labors and He models that for us in Genesis.

Genesis 2:1-3
Thus the heavens and the earth were completed in all their vast array.
2 By the seventh day God had finished the work he had been doing; so on the seventh day he rested from all his work. 3 Then God blessed the seventh day and made it holy, because on it he rested from all the work of creating that He had done.

He showed us by His example what a healthy relationship looked like. He worked hard and then took time to reflect and rest. The New Testament shows us many examples of Jesus separating from the crowd and resting even though He had a major job to do. He needed to disconnect and rest even when the salvation of the world was resting on His shoulders. This is the way that the Gospel of Mark tells the story of calming the sea.

Mark 4:35-40.

That day when evening came, He said to His disciples, "Let us go over to the other side." Leaving the crowd behind, they took Him along, just as He was, in the boat. There were also other boats with Him. A furious squall came up, and the waves broke over the boat, so that it was nearly swamped. Jesus was in the stern, sleeping on a cushion. The disciples woke Him and said to Him, "Teacher, don't you care if we drown?"
He got up, rebuked the wind and said to the waves, "Quiet! Be still!" Then the wind died down and it was completely calm. He said to His disciples, "Why are you so afraid? Do you still have no faith?"

Here is what I love about this passage: Jesus sees that there is work to be done. He sees the crowd. He knows people need to be healed, demons need to be cast out, and lessons need to be taught. But He still tells His disciples to get in the boat, and once there, He falls asleep. Yes, the needs of the people are urgent, and their requests (or cries) for healing must have been compelling, but Jesus knows that He needs to stop and rest.

If even Jesus needs to stop and rest in the midst of a chaotic world, with all of the important things He had to do, don't you think we need rest, too? I think we need to follow His example and set boundaries on our time, in order to live lives full of what we were *meant* to do, not what we think we're *supposed* to do. Setting boundaries in our lives is the only way to ensure we stay healthy: physically, mentally, and spiritually.

God calls us to put our lives in order and to put everything in its proper place. People need a day to reflect, meditate, contemplate, and turn their eyes inward rather than outward. I challenge you to take a step back from your material pursuits and look at life from a different perspective.

There is a great story of Jesus visiting His friends Mary and Martha that affirms this point.

Luke 10:38-42

38 As Jesus and his disciples were on their way, he came to a village where a woman named Martha opened her home to him. 39 She had a sister called Mary, who sat at the Lord's feet listening to what he said. 40 But Martha was distracted by all the preparations that had to be made. She came to him and asked, "Lord, don't you care that my sister has left me to do the work by myself? Tell her to help me!" 41 "Martha, Martha," the Lord answered, "you are worried and upset about many things, 42 but few things are needed—or indeed only one.Mary has chosen what is better, and it will not be taken away from her."

As Martha hurries to ensure the preparations, Mary simply sits at the feet of Jesus and listens to the wisdom of Christ. Martha then says to Jesus, "Lord, don't you care that my sister has left me to do the work by myself? Tell her to help me!" Jesus replies, "Martha, Martha, you are worried and upset about many things, but only one thing is needed. Mary has chosen what is better, and it will not be taken away from her."

Are you a Mary or a Martha? Are you so busy with your lists of things to accomplish that you forget that God is sitting in your living room. Mary sat in the Lord's presence while Martha was present but not in the presence of her Lord, she was too busy banging pots. It's not that preparing the meal and doing the endless chores that need to get done while maintaining your home aren't important, it is just that sometimes pausing and allowing God to sit with you is more important.

Sometimes, I feel like life resembles a run-on sentence that is missing some much needed punctuation. We seem to be running from one event to another and there never seems to be enough time in the day do accomplish all that needs to get done. Frankly, there just isn't time for a break. God challenges us to change and to put ***"commas"*** and ***"semicolons"*** into our lives and occasionally a good old ***"period."*** He wants us to disconnect from the rat race and refresh ourselves. He challenges us to sit at His feet, to take time to be with friends, to slow down enough to listen to your child and to go out on a date with your spouse. We need to take a breath and regroup just as God did. It allows us to keep our life in balance and helps us identify when we are doing too much. Throughout the Gospels, we see that Jesus spent time with those He loved. Sure, He was busy healing and preaching but He also went to weddings, hung out with His friends, and visited with His family. Jesus was a man who not only understood the importance of spending time with those He loved but He modeled it throughout His life. He also knew the importance of taking care of himself. He knew when to disconnect and regroup. That meant that sometimes he needed to turn away from those who needed Him because He was human as well and knew that He needed to refresh Himself.

There is a beautiful hymn written by Horatio Spafford in 1873 after some dramatic events occurred in his life. The first was the death of his four year old son and the second was the Great Chicago Fire of 1871, which ruined him financially since he had invested heavily in property that was damaged. Just when he felt he couldn't experience anymore heartache he sent his family to Europe ahead of him as he finished up his business dealings. The ship the *SS Ville du Havre* collided with a sea vessel, the *Loch Earn* and all four of Spafford's daughters died. His wife Anna survived and sent a telegram with the simple and tragic words **"Saved alone ..."** As he traveled by ship to be at his wife's side he wrote a hymn as the vessel passed where his daughters perished. He called his hymn "Ville du Havre" after the ship that sank or the title that many of us know is "It Is Well, With My Soul". The trials that he encountered were overwhelming and yet he was still able to say "It is well, with my soul" and praised the Lord. That, my friend, is great faith.

Life is tough and trials will come. Some will be harder to deal with than others but God promises that He will be with you in your boat if you just invite him.

When my children's Kindergarten teacher was diagnosed with a brain tumor I sent her a note and a bag of Lifesavers. I told her that

God would be beside her and that she could rest knowing that He held her safely in His arms. She passed away a few weeks later and when I went to her wake I was introduced to her husband. I told him that my children's love for learning was cultivated by having her as their Kindergarten teacher. I also mentioned that I wasn't sure if she received it or not but I sent her some Lifesavers. As I said this a tear floated down his cheek and he reached into his pocket. He pulled out a handful of Lifesavers and told me that they got my message and that currently, they were keeping him afloat. I was touched and thankful that I sent their family something concrete to hold on to during this storm in their life.

I challenge you to tell your children about the importance of having God as a Lifesaver in their lives and the significance of the candy Lifesaver. Then when you child is going through a storm or overwhelmed with a burden you can gently slip them a Lifesaver and remind them that they aren't alone. God will hold them up and allow them to rest in His presence. What a wonderful comforting thought. **Proverbs 3:5-6** Trust in the Lord with all your heart, and do not lean on your own understanding. In all your ways acknowledge him, and he will make straight your paths.

CHAPTER 6

Prepare Them For The Journey

~·~

S ailing is a sport where you can't just jump in a boat one day and
take off. Before you can cast away from the shoreline you need
to understand the dynamics of sailing, have an understanding of the
wind direction and you need to be sure that you have the tools on
board to help you in an emergency. The preparation to set sail takes
time and thought. Likewise it is important to spend time preparing
your child for their eventual journey away from the comfort of the
safe harbor. I am always amazed when I talk to parents and they
haven't taught their children how to function in the world before
they leave the nest. I see kids that are 18 years old that have never
done laundry or cooked a meal. They don't know how to manage
their money and have never had to use their own money to buy
things. They have been sheltered into thinking that everything mag-
ically gets done for them. When it is time to leave home they are ill
equipped to know how to do the simplest of acts. It is important
to train a child while they are under your care so that when they do
leave home they are equipped to navigate the new environment that
they will be living in.

I ran the junior sailing program for five years and before any of
the kids went out to sail for the first time they had to complete a
swim test. This included having them tread water for five minutes

and then putting on their lifejacket while they were in the water. We wanted them to know that they were strong enough to be on their own for a few minutes until someone could get to them. Also, it's very different putting a lifejacket on when they were on dry land verses trying to put one on while they were in the water. We wanted them to know that they had done it before and if a situation occurred, they could do it again. Likewise, teaching your child some basic skills empower them to have confidence that they can tackle problems that they may encounter. If they are never given the opportunity to challenge themselves while they are under your watch they may not have the confidence to know what they are capable of doing.

Next, we taught them how to balance the boat. How to adjust their weight to keep the boat steady, especially if they got hit with a big wave or a puff of wind. A minor adjustment could keep the boat stable but if they overcompensated they could cause the boat to capsize. Our number one goal was to run a safe program and the way to do that was by slowly and steadily develop confidence in them. They learned about boat balance and that would be vital for every other lesson during the summer. Helping your children understand the importance of a balanced life is something that should be taught in the home. We all know the importance of a balanced diet, but there are other areas that need the same attention. Time management helps your child understand the need to dedicate time to school, work, play and rest. If they focus too much time in one area, other areas in their life may suffer. By being attentive to how your child manages their time allows you the opportunity to teach some life lessons that they will use for their entire life.

When raising children it is important to begin early to teach them vital lessons that will allow them to manage their own journey. You are preparing them to leave the nest one day and that preparation needs to be on ongoing process. Chores are an important tool to help with their development. Why is it important to have your kids help around the house, especially when it is easier and less of a hassle sometimes to do it yourself? Because it is never too early to let them know that something is expected of them. Clearing the table can begin as early as two with having them bring their plate to the kitchen counter. Eventually, you can have them help with meal prep and then with the actual shopping. It is a great way to help them learn how to navigate a store and all that is involved with simple meal preparation. I use to have my kids take a week in the summer and plan the menu and not only do the shopping but prepare the meals for the family during that given week. I gave them a budget to work with and then I would take them shopping. It was their choice whether I would go around with them or hang out in the magazine aisle and wait for them to be finished on their own. They could look through cookbooks and plan a new meal or go with just spaghetti and jar sauce. They had to look through the cabinet to see what supplies they needed and they were allowed to buy the snacks for the week. I will tell you that today my kids are all great cooks and my daughter in laws have made a point to thank me since my boys not only know how to cook but take pride in their cooking. It took time and effort but I prepared them for the next chapter in their lives.

When they make their bed in the morning they learn that before the day fully begins they have accomplished something. A made bed also brings a sense of peace and order to their world. If you don't make your bed, try it for a week and see if you don't find your bedroom more peace-filled and a little bit calmer.

When they set the table they learn how to serve. When they clear the table they learn that they need to pick up after themselves. If they don't do their chore, such as setting the table after you've asked them ten times, the worst mistake you can make is to go ahead and do it for them. The child learns that if they just outlast you they can get away with not doing it. My solution is to put the food on the table and just sit there with no silverware or dishes. Your food may get cold but your child will learn that when they don't do their job, everyone suffers.

Our kids also learned how to manage their money at an early age. We never gave them gas money unless they were traveling to or from school or college, otherwise, that tank of gas was on them. If they wanted to go on a date they used their own money or learned how to find free things to do. They bought their own car (with a bit of help from us) but they learned how to take care of it since it was their own money that was invested. We paid for their car insurance unless they got a traffic ticket and then the insurance was on them for a year. If they abused the traffic laws then there would be a consequence. If they didn't have the money, then they didn't drive their car or they worked at a job to pay off the debt. They needed to learn the value of obeying the laws.

The other tool that I used was the "Saturday Box." I didn't use it often but when I did, it meant business. I would forewarn them that I was pulling out the Saturday box and before they went to bed I expected them to put their things away. If any of their items were left out and I had to pick it up, then it went into the box and they didn't see it until Saturday. I didn't care if it was shoes, Legos or their jacket. If I picked it up after the warning, it was gone. How empowering for me to know that I wasn't going to trip over Legos for a few days and I was actually glee filled knowing that the argument of telling them to put their things away was gone until Saturday.

I read the story of a mom who took a clear Tupperware and wrote on it:

TOY JAIL

You left it out and I picked it up, I've got your stuff, you're out of luck. To get it back, please do a chore, then it's yours, just like before. Love, Mom

The reason that I took this responsibility so seriously was that I wanted my kids to have the tools that they needed when they cast off into the open seas. I wanted them to have the confidence to be able to handle what came their way. Because I knew that I couldn't prepare them for all of the trials out there, I could at least prepare them for the ones that I knew they would experience. The idea of being able to care for oneself and keep their head above water.

An issue that I see parents making is being a helicopter parent (hovering over them all the time) or now it is common to see lawn mower parenting (mowing down the problems for the kids so they don't have to face them). Both are tremendously damaging to a child even though parents have the best of intentions.

Helicopter Parenting... I'm sure you've seen it. Parents who hover and don't allow their kids the opportunity to solve their own problems or even experience any trials. Today, with cell phones so prevalent, kids call home with every little problem and don't learn how to figure things out for themselves. I call it a long umbilical line. It is time to cut the cord when you see your kids reaching out to you to solve the simplest of problems. When your kids can't make decisions, or don't feel safe unless you can be reached, then you know that you have a problem. I know that as parents we love to feel needed and having our kids check in all the time feels great but you need to reflect on who is steering the boat? Are you still holding the tiller for them or do they feel confident enough to take over the helm? Remember our goal is to make them independent, self-sufficient, responsible adults. We want them to feel confident to cast away and leave the safety of the harbor. This is their journey and not a time for us to hold too tightly to the bow line.

Lawn Mower Parenting ... The desire to prevent our children from ever having to experience failure or disappointment. Parents plow down anything and everything that may cause their child to be upset. Parents want to make sure everyone plays fair, they want their child's teachers to know how "special" they are, and they want coaches who wouldn't think of not playing their child. They don't want their children to ever experience failure. The problem with this way of parenting is that the whole purpose of childhood is to fail. When a baby wants to start walking, they first have to fall and do it a lot. When they want to learn how to ride a bike they have to learn that gravity has consequences. If they have friends over and other kids want to play with their toys, then they have to learn how to share. They go to school and have to learn that getting along with others isn't that easy. Kids pick teams, coaches play favorites, teachers don't always grade on curves. Basically life isn't fair! The point of life is not to ride through the journey without any scars but to learn how to pick oneself up after the fall and keep on going. We want to help kids learn from their mistakes and gain wisdom. I always tell parents that there is value in letting kids fail, especially when they are small and the falls are close to the ground. If you protect your child from the little falls then they won't be prepared for the bigger ones. The hurt is much greater when the falls are big. If they learn the consequences of an F on a paper in fifth grade, it's upsetting but not as damaging as getting an F as a senior that may keep them out of their desired college. All falls hurt but the damage from a bigger fall is greater and can have lasting damage.

Help them become students of themselves.

As I mentioned before, one of the challenges of growing a little person and guiding them to become an adult is to help them understand who they are. What are their strengths and what are their weaknesses? What talents are they born with and what talents can they cultivate? Too often we think of our kids as a smaller version of ourselves and therefore limit their potential because we don't see it. Each of us are born with certain traits and gifts that need to be cultivated in order to see their true potential. Certain traits go hand in hand with a person's life calling. Someone who is good in math may choose a career as an accountant, an analytical person may choose engineering, and a compassionate soul may gravitate toward medicine. But becoming a student of our children goes beyond their career choices and involves more of getting to know who they are as a person. Helping them to be their best selves and then challenge them to bring out the best in those around them.

A child's birth order may also impact who they are. According to Dr. Kevin Leman who wrote "The Book Order Book," a first born is usually a high achiever and they may gravitate toward a job that requires precision, strong concentration and mental discipline such as science, law, engineering or medicine. They are usually highly motivated to achieve and have a tendency to be overly responsible. First borns have a tendency to be uptight because mom and dad were probably either overprotective, anxious, tentative, inconsistent or strict. As parents they may have used a demanding disciplined approach and encouraged their children to perform better. The majority of people who get counseling are first born or only children. They carry the weight of responsibility on their shoulders and that load can get heavy.

A middle child has a tendency to be a maverick. They forge their own way and love a good challenge. There are usually not a lot of pictures of them alone. You may notice that they tend to have lots of friends as they usually seek their approval for their affirmation. They have a desire to be independent and are extremely loyal to their peers. They usually leave home first and find bonding outside the family since they may have felt left out because they were squeezed from above and below. They usually make great parents, as they know how to negotiate and love to solve problems.

The baby of the family is usually a charmer and knows how to manipulate others. They are affectionate, uncomplicated and sometimes absent minded. They also have a tendency to love the limelight. They are usually the clown of the family and don't take life too seriously. They want people to notice them and they are considered a "people person" so they usually make good salespeople.

Having an understanding of birth order helps you to understand some of your child's behavior. Of course this is not true for every child but it does allow you to remember that your child's placement in the family does have some impact. Likewise, many times who your child is depends on what role is taken already. If the "high achiever" role is taken then the next child might find their place as the "athlete" or the "family clown". Everyone wants a place all their own in the family and if one role is taken they may find another role to fill. I was the third born but also the baby for 11 years until my little brother was born. I found that my role was the responsible one. My mother always said that if she asked me to do something like clean the kitchen, I would usually get it done.

My brother and sister would typically not do the chore so my sense of affirmation came from wanting to please and complete the task.

The point that I would like to make is to spend some time watching the dynamics in your home. Try to gain some wisdom into who your kids are and how they see themselves. My youngest child never had an opinion. If I asked him what he wanted for breakfast he was so easygoing that he would say that it didn't matter. If we were going out to eat and I asked where he wanted to go he usually responded with "Wherever you want to eat, mom." I realized that as he got older this behavior would start to become a problem. Yes, he is a tremendously happy and easygoing kid but I wanted him to learn to have a voice. I made a point to ask his opinion and I expected an answer. He needed to get off the fence and chose a side. He needed to learn to trust himself and pick a direction. If I wasn't paying attention I might have missed that it was becoming a problem. He is still delightfully easygoing but at least now when I ask him a question, I get an answer. Today he is an engineer and successfully following his own path. He lives the furthest from home and I think he needed to make his own way and get out from the shadow of his siblings.

One of the things that I really enjoyed when my children started to head off to college was to watch the dynamics in my home when the eldest left and my second born was now in the limelight away from his sister's shadow. I got to watch him come into his own and really thrive. He became more confident and independent. It was exciting to watch the transformation from little brother to the oldest in the home ... at least until his sister returned from college. I realized that he loved this new stage and it was interesting to watch as his sister fully expected him to be the same little boy that she left behind. That was not to be. He now had a new standing in the home and wasn't going to pushed aside. It didn't take them long to readjust to the new dynamics but it did require some growth on everyone's part. The same growing opportunity occurred when he went away to college and the third got his chance to shine in the limelight.

I have enjoyed each and every stage that my kids went through but some stages are certainly tougher than others. It is helpful to have some basic growth and development knowledge to help parents understand what the different stages are. Of course we have all heard about the terrible twos and certainly junior high has its road bumps that we need to anticipate. It is important to identify challenging behaviors and evaluate them. Parents need to do a periodic assessment to see if a child's behavior is a stage that they are going through or are they developing a character flaw. By understanding what is normal developmental behavior we can evaluate whether our child is behaving appropriately or if they are veering toward a character flaw. If a child is possessive of their things and they are three, that's a stage. If they hit someone who is playing with their toy, that is a character flaw. It is important to be able to know the difference so that you can help shape your child and build their character.

It takes time to help in the creation of a masterpiece. There was a sculptor who created world famous statues. He would chisel away at a granite rock for days until it became a statue of a beautiful horse. When asked about his skills and how he knew how to create such a magnificent piece he responded that he just removed everything that wasn't a horse.

Our job as parents is to remove everything that isn't a healthy and responsible person. When we see sharp edges in their personality we chisel away until that sharp edge is smoothed out. If your child is disrespectful, then it is our job to teach them the importance of respect. If they are selfish then we need to teach them the value of thinking of others. It is a slow and tiring job but you will reap the benefits as you watch your child grow.

If you ever had a rock tumbler you might remember that you put these jagged stones into the tumbler and turned it on. That thing needed to tumble for days and days. It probably started out in your kitchen but before nightfall it found its way to the garage, for it was constant and noisy. (Sounds a bit like a teenager doesn't it?) Eventually, you opened up the tumbler and there was a gemstone. It takes time and lots and lots of patience to cultivate a beautiful gemstone from a jagged rock. That is also true with raising your children.

Once, when one of my sons got into trouble at school, I had to meet with the headmaster. My son pulled a prank on his friend and was caught and I was in the office to hear of the consequences for his actions. I assured the headmaster that I would take care of it but I also needed to remind him that I had a "Simon" and I was growing him to become a "Peter." That takes time! (The apostle Peter was originally called Simon and Jesus changed his name to Peter which meant "rock" before he was worthy to have that name. Jesus saw his potential and knew that the church would one day be built on his shoulders.) The challenge for us is to see that potential in our own children.

The last step when taking the stone out of the rock tumbler is to polish it and allow the gem to shine. Before the wedding of my son I gave a speech to my future daughter in law. I told her that I spent my son's lifetime watching him in the rock tumbler. He had some sharp edges and imperfections that needed to be smoothed out, but today I was giving her a gemstone. I wanted to thank her as her presence in his life polished him to a perfect shine, for she brought out the best in him. As I welcomed her into our family I also let her know that I have been praying for her since the day my son was born. I prayed that one day he would find a life partner whom he could share his life journey with and would bring out the best in him. On his wedding day I got to watch him truly shine.

The challenge for the sculptor is to have steady hands. To be accurate with their chisel and bold with their strikes. The same care must be employed with parenting. It is important to shape the child but not crush their spirit. There is a delicate balance and it is especially challenging if we have lots of sharp edges ourselves which causes us to be a bit shaky. If we have baggage that influences how we parent and causes us to overreact or ignore things that need addressing, then we may have trouble with our finished product.

Over and over again as I teach classes about parenting, the parents all slowly come to the realization that most of parenting is about getting their own act together. Realizing their own areas of weaknesses or discovering old wounds that they may have, will allow them to begin to heal themselves. The process of being a good parent begins with self-discovery and an honest evaluation of not only our past but what our future expectations are as well. To become a wisdom seeker. It is also important to have a conversation with their spouse about what their background, wounds, and expectations are so that they can both approach this demanding chapter with under-standing and wisdom. The process may involve forgiving some issues from their past, letting go of unhealthy relationships with their own parents or lowering some unrealistic expectations for themselves so that they can begin to handle the extensive job of parenting.

First, identify where you have an issue and then ask God for clarity and understanding. From there you can confess your weak-ness and ask God to build you up in that area and learn to "Let Go" of the burdens that are holding you back from being the best parent you can be. God is not expecting you to be perfect and He knows how hard the journey is. Remember He started this world with Adam and Eve and they rebelled against a perfect parent so be easy on yourself. When you finally lift it to prayer I am confident that you will experience a sense of peace and refreshment. Then daily, ask God to be beside you and guide you on this journey. He will in time empower you with the gifts of the Spirit: Love, Joy, Peace, Patience, Kindness, Goodness, Faith, Gentleness and Self-Control ... Gal. 5:22. Notice I keep coming back to this verse because these fruits are available to all of us.

I definitely didn't start this parenting chapter of my life with a lot patience or self-control. One day I was so frustrated that I swept everything off a table and broke a wooden Christmas figure. Once my rage subsided I was heartbroken that my kids witnessed my behavior and that my reaction was so violent that I broke some-thing that I cherished. But the blessing that came out of my reaction was that I knew that I needed help. It was then that I started going to Bible Study and joined a parenting group. I became proactive in my pursuit of parenting. I listened to Christian radio, and inspirational speakers. I prayed ... a lot! Slowly but surely I saw a change in me and as a result a change in my children and my home. I have such peace and a patience that I never knew I was capable of. I was growing fruit. I needed a new model from that which I had grown up with and I made a decision to change the legacy of my home. I gained control over my life and as a result I watched my kids gain a control over theirs. I learned to enjoy each chapter they went through and nothing thrilled me more than to spend time in their presence. It became the home that the neighborhood kids all came to and I cherished that. I brought fun, safety, and wisdom into our home. It was a safe harbor. I will never regret the decision to ask God into our home and have Him guide us all on our journey.

As I reflect on parenting I think it is a lot like planting a garden. One day you are given a seed, and you are filled with excitement at its potential. You begin the process of tilling the soil and preparing the earth to accept that seed. Daily you watch as it grows until one day it sprouts and breaks free of the binding soil. You are overjoyed! Now you watch to see if it needs more sun or if it's too dry and needs some water. Sometimes you are concerned that you watered it too much or the sun is too bright and it needs a bit of shade for the day. Each seed's requirements are different and your job as the gardener is to know each seed and what its needs are. It takes time and lots and lots of patience. Then one day you go out into your garden and you see this leggy, tall thing that doesn't look anything like the picture on the seed package. What the heck is this? Is this a weed? Did I do something wrong? But being a good gardener you keep taking care of it and make sure it has enough water and sunlight. And then one day something miraculous happens. Where that tall stem was, you now see that it has bloomed into a beautiful flower and stands on its own. It brings a joy to your heart that you never knew you were capable of experiencing. You get to see the fruits of your labor and delight in its product. You learned the lesson that you will reap what you sowed. You sowed a home of honor and respect, you taught your child how to navigate their own boat. You let them know that they have a lifesaver who will care for them. You cultivated their faith and you empowered them to be the best they could be. That, my friend, is parenting.

CHAPTER 7
Putting Your Team Together

~

N othing is more important when you are assembling a team than the selection of your teammates. These are the people that you band together with to achieve success. They do not necessarily have to be the most talented, but they need to understand their part and know how to work together to reach the desired goal.

Sailing can be a solo event but more often than not the boat requires a combination of other crew members to man the boat. Someone who has skills flying the spinnaker may not be the right person to go forward to do a sail change. Some people are great at calling the wind shifts and others are needed for their brute strength. Assembling a successful team requires a skipper who knows the strengths and weaknesses of his entire team and works to make them the best possible teammates.

I sail in a three-person boat. The skipper is on the tiller steering, managing the mainsail and calling tactics. The middle crew is responsible for trimming the jib (forward sail) along with flying the spinnaker (colorful sail) on the downward legs, and the forward crew manages the sail changes, boat adjustments and is constantly on the lookout for wind. Together we work as a team to sail at optimum speed as we navigate the course and battle against the other competitors. There is beauty in watching a well orchestrated team navigate around the racecourse. It begins with a battle for a good start as you jockey for the best position so that you can get off the starting line cleanly. This might require keeping the boat as flat as possible by hiking out to counter the push of the wind against the sail. Getting off the starting line with clear air can make all the difference as you are able to sail with a fresh breeze and not in another boat's bad air. Likewise, starting a family without a lot of baggage and unrealistic expectations can be the difference between a smooth start and one that is bogged down with dirty air. As you navigate the boat an attentive crew looks for changes around the race course and pays attention the the always changing conditions. Mark rounding can be vital in your race as the boat that makes the sail change quickly can pull ahead and get a fresh breeze. All of it requires teamwork and a beforehand knowledge of what needs to be done and who will be doing it.

Raising children requires that same team approach. If you sail singlehanded something may be missed, or just impossible to accomplish. You can't hoist a sail and steer the boat at the same time without losing ground and possibly hitting another vessel or capsizing. Likewise, you can't be all things to your child without consequences such as burn out or missing something important. Each child is unique and requires different skills as they navigate their life journey. They will be experiencing different stages in their life and with those stages come different challenges that need to be addressed.

When you approach child rearing with an understanding of this simple, yet vital concept, you allow your child to achieve a better outcome and you come through the process without burnout. The challenge is to put together a winning team.

The first concept about building a successful team is that you need to be able to work together. There may be adverse conditions ahead that require cool heads and if you begin with a team that is on edge then disaster may occur when the trials come. Raising a child requires a team approach with a united front. Having a trained crew who understands their roles and knows the importance of their job is important. It doesn't just happen, it takes planning, education and time to put together a winning team.

I council parents and I see the lack of good communication as the number one issue in many homes. Sometimes I find that they are both trying to be the skipper at the same time and as a result they are both directing the child but giving different orders. This creates confusion in the child's world. Sometimes I see parents talking *at* each other not *to* each other so that an understanding about the child's needs are not being heard. Or I may witness a selfishness on the part of one spouse as they are more concerned about themselves than what is best for the team. Sadly, in some situations, one parent may fail to show up altogether, which puts the child at a major disadvantage before they even leave the dock. The result in all these situations is that communication between team members is faulty so there is a lack of understanding about what needs to be done or who is going to do it. Sometimes there is no communication at all! If I were to put my finger on the one item that causes the most conflict in both the marriage and in child rearing it would be the simple issue of communication.

Communication ... the ability to convey your point clearly and with a common understanding about what needs to be done. I like to look at communication like playing a game of tennis where there is a rhythmic flow back and forth. Nothing is more frustrating than to serve the ball and have the other team member not hit it back. In order to enjoy a good volley you need to keep your eye on the ball and watch it connect with the racket to send the ball back. Too often I see one partner distracted and not really into the game so they don't send the ball back or send it back in such a way that it isn't a hittable shot for the other partner. There is no flow, there is no communication, and there is no fun. Other times I see one partner try to slam the ball back so hard that you couldn't possible return the volley. Frustration builds and before long one partner leaves the field of play because they feel like they are in a game of "gotcha."

I once brought a group of kids to the local tennis court to teach them how to play tennis. As I let them go at it there was total chaos.

Balls were flying everywhere as their goal was to hit the ball so that the other person couldn't hit it back. It wasn't pretty and it wasn't fun. Too many balls went flying outside the fence and there was just chaos on the court. I stopped everyone and told them to change the way they were playing the game. Eventually, there would be a time to play aggressively but not when you are learning the game. So I had everyone pair up and now their goal would be to see which team could put together the most volleys. Do you know what happen? Order came over the courts, the kids started playing like a team and they worked together to make sure that the other person was successful. They learned how to volley and they had fun doing it. They learned how to play the game and realized that it was enjoyable. They developed an understanding that for them to be successful their partner needed to be successful as well.

When you are with someone whom you connect with, the flow is just there. The conversation goes back and forth, the relationship is stimulating and everyone feels good. The flow of conversation is easy and there is an understanding about what the other person needs to be successful. There isn't the need to play "gotcha" and look for ways to slam the other person. If someone is off mark with a return there is a grace that allows the other person to have a do over. An understanding is there because the goal is clear: for both partners to be successful.

To learn how to communicate it is important to understand that each team member has different skills. It is so easy to volley with a dear friend because usually they are like you and you have common beliefs and ideas. But when you get married you are teaming with someone who may be totally different. Their background and how they were raised may not line up with your expectations. Their idea of how to discipline a child may be influenced by how they were disciplined and for better or worse they may want to change things. When couples get married their role changes from being "self-centered" to "we-centered" as they are now part of a team. That adjustment can be hard for some people. There are expectations, jobs that need to be done, pressures that come from added responsibilities and then add to that the major changes that occur when children enter the picture and you can have the workings of major strife. Once a baby enters into your world everyone's role changes. Husbands now take on the added responsibilities of being a father and instead of coming home to his wife he is coming home to someone's mother. Wives may feel overwhelmed and exhausted with the responsibility of providing, caring and management of the home and a new baby. Add to that the need to go back to work and the stress level can be off the chart.

Parenthood takes on a new perspective and not only do husbands and wives change with their new role of mom and dad but the new grandparents go through a role change as well. These changes occur during the overwhelming time of caring for a newborn complete with sleepless nights and raging hormones. Before long your world has changed and you really didn't have a say in those changes.

Parenting requires you to see beyond yourself and transfer a *selfish* attitude into a *selfless* one. That can be quite frustrating for some people who didn't realize that this change needed to occur. They feel victimized by the situation and frustrated that they don't see a way out. When they keep these feelings bottled up, stress results and with stress the need to blame someone else for their unhappiness. This happens slowly but with time it can undermine a perfectly good marriage and change a teammate into an enemy.

Most of the major issues can be resolved with some time spent cultivating communication and understanding. By developing a desire to help the other person to be successful and to work hard at maintaining a good volley the team can eventually develop a rhythm that works for them. When your focus is to bring out the best in your teammate, you can both learn to be successful in all areas of your life. You can't volley alone, so it is vital that you help the other person play to the best of their ability. My goal as a spouse is to help my husband be the best that he can be. To encourage, support, and understand what his needs are. Oh, I am not always successful but more often than not we have learned to volley well. We encourage each other, we take turns at stepping up and we share the responsibility of the game. It needs to be done constantly, and when we have an off day we are able to shake it off and try again tomorrow. We don't look at changing partners as an option. We don't consider embarrassing our teammate and we don't throw a hissy fit on the court. We are committed teammates who will lift the other one up when they are having an off day and strive for greatness whenever we can.

When you pay attention to your relationships, you may notice that some conversations just happen easily and without effort and others require more attention and care. When talking to your best friend you may spend an hour on the phone and still have plenty to say when you hang up, yet when talking to your spouse you may get a few words in before they zone out. That doesn't mean that that conversation is any less valuable, it's just different. There needs to be an understanding about the way each relationship works. If you are looking for your spouse to be everything for you, you may be frustrated when they can't serve all your needs. The need for friends outside of the home can be vital for the health of your marriage as that serves a different purpose for your well being.

It is important to have an understanding of the difference between men and women. On average, men have a tendency to speak fewer words during a given day than women. Their need to communicate may be focused on getting to the problem and moving on. When they engage in a conversation their goal may be to get to the bottom line. They may have spent all of their words at work so when they get home their focus is to just chill and enjoy the quiet. Home may be their place to escape from the stresses they experienced all day. Some men, and women as well, may just need a few minutes to regroup before they can fully change modes and engage in the home life.

Women, on the other hand, have a tendency to be more vocal and typically use more words on a given day. They are usually more relational and their identity is wrapped up in the people in their lives while a man usually identifies their success by their career.

This basic understanding can resolve a lot of common problems in a home. Their needs aren't wrong they are just different.

A good way to understand the differences between men and women is to think of a string of Christmas tree lights. A man can be like the light strand with the big bulbs. When one light goes out they can still function but women have a tendency to be more like the Christmas tree lights that if one goes out they all go out. If she isn't feeling good with parenting, her lights may go out in the bedroom. If she is hurting with a friendship issue she is hurting at home as well. Her success is based on the health of her relationships, while men's successes are based on their role in the world.

An example of the differences between men and women can also be found with their need to communicate. As I mentioned before, women typically have the need to use more words in a given day compared to a man who usually is less vocal. (Be aware that these are general trends and differ from person to person.) If a mom is home all day with a toddler she has had very little chance to use her words. Her words have been stored up and she is waiting to use them as soon as her spouse walks through the door. If he is zoned out because of a problem at work, she feels rejected and undervalued when he isn't interested in talking. Immediately, communication is impacted and frustration and hurt may result. Both have needs and at that given moment neither are being met. A simple "Honey, give me 10 minutes to regroup as it's been a really long day." or "The kids have been driving me crazy and I really need to talk. Let me know when you can give me some of your time." Both examples allow the one person to have some space but also the reassurance that when the time is right needs will be met. Understanding the other person's needs and makeup help resolve many of these problems.

Because of the changes in the job force and our social fabric, many women are becoming working moms and dads are helping with more of the family duties. Lines that were once traditional have now changed. Single households are more common, same-sex relationships may raise a family, grandparents may be bringing up their grandkids, and some families live thousands of miles from any family support. All of these situations require good lines of communication to help the family to become successful.

MARK ROUNDINGS

When you are sailing, it is vital that your team learns how to work together or you can have chaos in the boat, especially at a mark rounding. Everyone has a job to do and if done well it can make the difference from a clean rounding to total disaster. It is vital that the skipper is able to keep their eyes outside of the boat to ward off any potential disaster or unexpected situation. If the skipper doesn't trust the forward crew to execute their job then their focus may be on what the forward crew is doing rather than their own responsibilities. The result is that the skipper isn't prepared for the challenges that may come at the mark rounding. The entire boat suffers and it can impact the success of the team. It is a challenge to work together when the situation is calm and predictable, but add some tense moments like the start of a race or a mark rounding and then tensions rise, and attacks occur.

It is important to have that understanding when you are parenting. Everyone has a job to do and knowing what those jobs are can make a big difference when the situation inside the home gets tense. Everyone needs to have a clear understanding of their roles and then the parents can work together for the common good of the family. When a mark rounding occurs such as a family move, career changes, an illness, the change from middle to high school, and the like, clear communication has been cultivated so now everyone knows what their job is. Each parent has an understanding of what is expected of them and that helps transitions go a bit smoother. Communication and an understanding about expectations help everyone to feel more confident and then they know how to properly manage the change in course so the outcome is beneficial to all of the family members.

In parenting, teamwork is vital for a successful outcome. Even when parents disagree it is important to present a united front and work together for the common good so that your child doesn't have the opportunity to pit one parent against another. To develop an understanding ahead of time who will be doing what jobs and how those jobs should be done needs to be discussed before the challenges of tense situations occur. Sharing the burdens of child rearing, especially as your children enter into the teenage years, is important so that one spouse doesn't get overwhelmed or burnt out. This is an important time for fathers to really step up and get involved especially if they have let mom handle the kids prior to puberty. A male role model is vital for both the sons and the daughters in their development. As a matter of fact there is a bit of a male crisis due to the absence of fathers in their son's lives. Overwhelmingly, the male population in prisons are from men whose fathers were absent in the homes. They account for an increase in violence, drug use and mass shootings. They need a father figure to guide, nurture, and direct them so that they may be held accountable for their actions. Even if the parents are divorced, it is important to have dad in the picture to help during this critical time in a child's life. Many young girls will look at their relationship with their father to base who they will date and eventually marry. If the father is abusive, or absent they may settle for that in their male relationships. A young girl tends to seek approval from a male figure if her father has been absent and that may lead to risky behavior. If a father is absent, then enlisting a grandfather or an uncle to step in to be that male role model may be helpful.

Communication within your team is vital as you want to establish healthy relationships and common goals. Whatever your circumstances, assess what your options are and see if you can put together a winning team even if it is a bit ragtag. The goal is to help your children develop healthy relationships, that can contribute to growth in wisdom and maturity.

Working as a team leads to the health of the family. If the children are on a steady footing they can proceed with confidence through the stages that they have to go through. They will learn and understand that relationships require teamwork and communication. As they mature they will then look for relationships of their own that model health. When they see you navigating stormy conditions and trials with a clear direction and an understanding of how you want to get through the situation it brings peace and comfort to the home. There is a clear order and understanding of what the goals are and how to reach them. If a situation arrises that is overwhelming, the team works together to find a solution. They trust each other and know how to problem solve so that they can have a successful outcome.

There also must be a clear chain of command. There is only one skipper at a time sailing a boat. Every position is valuable and needed but if the other crew members constantly undermine the skipper, then the boat in essence will not move forward. There will be mutiny onboard and leadership is gone. Likewise, if the skipper constantly devalues their crew members, then the team fails to perform and no one is doing their job. Conflict, blaming and discontentment will result. If you ever had an opportunity to watch a mark rounding in a sailboat race you can see this play out. Even though everyone started at the same time the lead boats usually have a team that knows how to work together, communicates efficiently and execute their jobs. They make it to the first mark ahead of the other competitors and as they round the mark their sail changes are immediate, they make the necessary adjustments with ease and little conflict, and they quickly are taking advantage of the wind and sailing away from their competition. It is a challenging time in a sailboat race, yet the winning boats navigate it with barely a word spoken. Everyone knows their job and they execute it with precision. Their spinnaker goes up immediately so they can take advantage of its power and they sail efficiently away from the pack. As you watch the boats who reach the mark further back you see less efficiency, more chaos, and definitely more yelling. The jobs aren't clearly defined and the crew isn't completely sure what to do next. Spinnakers go up tangled or take a long time to rise. The skipper needs to instruct and as a result his eyes are in the boat and not looking around him. He gets into trouble with other boats and sets himself up for challenges as he now has to ward off the bad air that the wind shadows from other boats cast. He spends all of his energy on the next leg fighting off trouble and trying to find his own clear lane. They end up getting further and further behind the lead boats and they spend more time trying to stay out of trouble then just looking for clear air to sail in.

I see many parents behave the same way. They don't prepare for the mark rounding that they know that their children will have to make; the change from toddler to school age, from grammar school to junior high and then on to high school. These are changes that will come whether you are ready or not. If you aren't prepared for those changes, then you will truly have your hands full when the teenage years arrive and you feel overwhelmed. Your team isn't in place and you aren't prepared to experience all the drama that comes with that stage. If parents aren't anticipating the changes then the result is that they aren't prepared and that may lead to disaster. They always seem to be playing catch up and they find themselves in situations with their kids that could have been avoided if they just got their eyes outside the boat and look around.

Many parents don't know what to look for and are shocked when they encounter a mark rounding and they aren't sure what to do. They forgot to train their teams or even assembled one to help during these changes. They haven't invested in their kids so they don't know who they are and what their needs are. They don't know their children's friends or what their interests are. Their children don't know how to perform basic life skills like doing their laundry, working at an entry level job or managing money. They aren't having the conversations needed with their kids about their future and as a result I see many kids floundering out of high school. They rounded the mark and don't have a clue where the wind is. They never had anyone invest in teaching them how to be successful and help get them on the road to becoming independent individuals. They don't understand who they are or what strengths they possess. Parents may find their child in bad air from drug use and now have to spend the rest of their lives fighting off the dirty air of that addiction. They don't soar because they weren't taught how.

Parents are too distracted with their own concerns that they ignore the problems when they could have been easily fixed and as a result they need to invest a lot more energy into just trying to keep their child going forward.

Have you ever seen a child who just seems to lag behind and when it is time to set their chute and sail away, they get caught at the mark and don't make any forward progress. They don't further their education with a college degree or trade school. They work at an entry-level job with no plans to take advantage of the winds and sail forward. They get distracted by a relationship that doesn't bring out the best in them and flounder or delay their development. You can't always protect them from having a bad mark rounding but you can equip them to learn from their experience and learn to not make the same mistakes at the next rounding.

Each child is different and each child is gifted with different abilities but all are called to set their sails and take advantage of the winds. The goal of the team members is to help make this happen. If no preparation is done beforehand then floundering will result. They will drift further and further behind the pack and limp slowly toward the finish line.

As parents, we have the opportunity to give our children the tools needed to be successful. We can begin by first and foremost being their "skipper" (parent). To be that lighthouse that stands tall and guides them on their journey. Not every boat is going to respond the same way and likewise not every child will respond the way you want them to. Remember it is their journey and they have the choice of how they are going to navigate their way on the open seas. But by paying attention to the details it helps each child to be their best and equips them with some of the tools that they will need for their journey. When you realize that you are preparing to send them off on their own into the open waters it makes it clear what you need to do. You can't wait to teach them at the last minute how to develop the skills that they will need to be safe and strong. It requires baby lessons geared to each chapter of their lives to help them to set their sails for their own journey.

Our family went white water rafting on the New River in West Virginia. Before we left the shore our guide instructed us about the importance of working as a team. We were going to be traveling down class IV and V rapids and it was important to work together to navigate the strong currents that would be sweeping us along. Most of the time we needed to make small adjustments to keep us in the flow of the river but sometimes we had to work really hard to prevent us from hitting some large boulders. The majority of the time you could just relax and let the currents float you down river but the guide knew where the dangers were and he prepared us ahead of time. We needed to get our feet under the straps and prepare for what lie ahead. At his direction he would have one side or the other "dig in!" What that meant was that we needed to use everything we had to paddle away from danger. To reach deep into the turbulent waters to direct the path of our boat. The sounds of the rushing water was overwhelming but I can still remember hearing him shouting "Dig in, dig in!" You couldn't help to do anything else but "dig in" for the safety of your boat depended on it. It didn't matter that you were tired, there would be rest afterward but in the middle of the rapids you were called to action. As parents we need to prepare our kids for the rapids that we know they will encounter. We need to challenge them to 'dig in" and direct their boat to steer away from dangers. We need to encourage them to work hard even when the challenges seem overwhelming.

When one of my sons was struggling in one of his classes he told me that the subject was too hard and the result was that his effort was minimal. I remember telling him that he needed to try twice as hard, not half as much. It was easy for him to let the subject overwhelm him and give up but that is when he needed to "dig in" and manage his boat. I encouraged him to ask for help and I kept on top of his grades to be sure he wasn't falling behind. He paired up with a friend to help him understand the work and eventually he came out with a passing grade. Digging in required effort and action and if your child drifts when they are in the hard part of their life they can very easily crash upon the imposing rocks that they will encounter. They can get discouraged and give up too easily.

We need to prepare them and then encourage them during the rapids of their life. "Dig in, dig in, dig in!" … that needs to be your call to your child to help them to be their best and avoid unnecessary crashes. The currents out there are strong and they are going to need everything they have to redirect their boat sometimes. Give them the tools and knowledge to do just that. Let them enjoy the thrill of accomplishments and the joy of a job well done.

THE CONDITION OF THE BOAT

Everyone would love to sail their journey in a beautiful new, fully rigged sailboat complete with a new set of sails. That really is every sailors dream but reality comes with a cost and many just can't afford that luxury. Some kids are born with the outward gifts that allow them an early advantage over some of their peers. They may have an athletic body, a gifted mind, or a musical ear. They don't have to work as hard to get the results they may want to achieve. But many a sailor, like many a child, have been successful with less than the best and that is because they have the best team.

My son came in second at the Nationals in sailing one year in an old boat, mediocre equipment, and an old set of sails. The first place boat was a world renown professional sailor who competes competitively for a living. My son was fresh out of college and he barely had enough money to enter the contest.

But, what advantage did he have over the other 80 competitors? He put a winning team together. He had his younger brother and his brother's future wife. Because he trusted his team members he could keep his eyes out of the boat and pay attention to the changing conditions around him. He could focus on boat speed, look around for wind, and observe what the other boats were doing. He trusted his team to manage the boat so he could focus on strategy. At mark roundings the sails went up effortlessly. If there was a snag, he trusted that his crew could handle it so he could pay attention to the direction he would sail. When he needed to focus on speed, he trusted his crew to be his eyes. They looked around and he trusted the information that they gave him. And do you know what probably led to their success more than anything... they had fun.

Too often I see parents miserable and as a result the home is filled with yelling and anger and they certainly don't understand the concept of working together. They don't think ahead and so they get blindsided by something that they should have seen coming. They don't trust their crew or they go out on the water shorthanded and then they try to do too much. They are always playing catch up and as a result the outcome is less than ideal.

Your child may not be the most gifted in any one area but with the right encouragement they can be successful and in many cases surpass their peers because they had a successful team behind them. What you can give them first and foremost is unconditional love. To give them the confidence to know that their parents not only love them but also like them. To help them know that at times they would need to "dig in" and work harder because things don't always come easily. They can learn to focus on their strengths which might be kindness, sportsmanship, or being a team player. They don't take themselves too seriously and learn how to have fun on the journey. Many times you can see the child that seems to "have it all" struggle when they aren't successful or someone else beats them. They can be arrogant in victory and ungracious in defeat. They can develop severe character flaws because of their "gifts" and as a result they can crash head first into rocks that so easily could be avoided.

As parents we need to teach our children that they are given one body for this journey called life. They may love it or hate it but it is theirs for the duration of their time on this earth. The sooner they come to embrace the vessel that they live in the sooner they can become a master of it. They can understand its strengths and accept its weaknesses. The challenge for many is that as parents we haven't learned this lesson and we are at constant battle with ourselves and we then model that to our children. We don't feed our mind, body and soul with good stuff and then wonder why our kids do the same thing. We invite smut into our homes by what we allow on our TVs, we indulge on junk food because it is easier, and we don't take time to invite God into our lives. We feel constant stress and then when our kids enter into challenging waters we get completely overwhelmed. We fail to enlist a supportive team and many times we actually do battle with our team members. We aren't prepared for the changes that will come and as a result there is chaos in the home.

So how do you put together a winning team? First and foremost, ask God to be your guide. He knows you completely and he knows your child and spouse. He will help guide you and bring you peace. He will let you know when it is time to "dig in" and when it is okay to rest. He knows the path and he will help you through the difficult times. Hear him call to you when the noise of the rapids are approaching and you will hear his voice above all that noise.

Besides asking God to lead your team, take a moment to evaluate who else you have in your life to bring about success. Did you get the A team? A family and friend support system that anticipates your family's needs and lifts up each member to be their best. If that is the case then good for you. If not, then training is required. The goal is to help everyone to be their best and realize their full potential. Too often in sailing I see a skipper completely berate their crew and then wonder why they aren't successful. Or they fail to take the time needed to train them and then wonder why they don't perform during the race.

WAYS TO BUILD A SUCCESSFUL TEAM

First ... spend time gaining knowledge. If you had wonderful role models growing up that led by example then you can observe and learn from their behavior. You were certainly blessed. Otherwise, you can look at homes that you want to emulate and watch how they treat each other. Find parents whom you admire and ask for their help. Go to the bookstore. There are wonderful resources out there that can help you gain knowledge and wisdom from experts who can help you on your journey. When you invest in gaining knowledge that will help you to understand your child, you will gain wisdom to guide them through various stages that they will experience. By gaining wisdom it will help you to not be blindsided by the changes they will be going through. By understanding stages, danger signs and ways to encourage and discipline your child it will power your light and allow your lighthouse to stand tall. Your ground will be steady and you'll keep your light burning. Be a wisdom seeker.

Second ... assemble your team. Your spouse plays and important part whether they are in the picture or not. In sailing, some boats sail with their spouse as I have done for over 40 years, but others realize that they can't sail together. The tension in the boat may be too great while sailing, yet many times they are a wonderful support team on the shore. Other times you see a boat that doesn't have a spouse involved at all. They are divorced from the situation and have no involvement whatsoever. You have to evaluate your own situation and the members that you have on your team. It is wonderful when you are both on the same page and you can work together to help your child on their journey. If you are divorced from the child's parent then you need to realize that regardless of the situation, that person will be a part of your child's life, and yours, for the rest of their life. You don't want your anger and bitterness to invade your child's life. The goal is to gain maturity and wisdom and to be an example for your child about what grace is. It doesn't mean that there aren't consequences for bad behavior or that you forget what harm's may have been done but by failing to let go of the bitterness you become a prisoner in your own world.

I had a friend who went through a very difficult chapter with her spouse when their children were still fairly young. She was hurting tremendously but she refocused and realized that her number one goal was to help the father be an important part of her children's life. It wasn't easy but she had enough wisdom to know that her children would need a relationship with him so she did everything she could, in spite of her pain, to cultivate that relationship. She maintained her character during the most difficult of circumstances and you know what she got out of it? Her children are beautiful and well adjusted kids. She also knew that she was going to need the support of a few close friends who were her "paper shredders." She could tell us what she was going through and how she was hurting. She could lay at our feet her wounds, and she was able to vent to us instead of her children. What she said to us went into the paper shredder. We allowed her to be raw, and honest as she worked through difficult things she was going through but we never bashed her husband and we didn't try to tell her what to do because ultimately the decisions needed to be hers. The whole world didn't need to know what her family was going through and as a matter of fact few people even knew there was trouble. That allowed her kids to be on more stable ground and avoid further injury.

Whatever your circumstances, try to have a heart-to-heart with your spouse about what the goals and expectations are for your child. Learn to anticipate the upcoming trials and be prepared for ways to navigate through them. I found that I served as the major support in my children's life when they were young but as they entered the teenage years they needed the support, and wisdom of their father. I needed to prepare him for this important role and encourage him to be successful. By addressing this as a united front, it allowed us to show our children strength and clarity. We helped them feel safe and allowed them to grow in maturity. If you can do that, you are one step closer to having a great team.

ASSEMBLING YOUR TEAM

Parenting is a tough job and it is vital to have some help so you don't experience burnout or get too distracted that you don't see the trouble that lies ahead. That is why it is important to assemble a team that can help you along the way.

The paper-shredders ...These are people that you can trust and that support you on your journey. As I mentioned before, having one or two friends that can serve as your paper shredders allows you to work through situations and verbalize your thoughts without the penalty of someone holding your words against you. This is not a gossip session, for that is where you gather to harm another person and spread false truths to wound another. This is where you have the luxury of being true to yourself and the few friends who know you and will support you. They allow you to be genuine without fear of them using what you said to hurt another person. These are rare people who earn this title through loyalty and dependability. They don't spread the information you shared and as a result they are invaluable.

Your back fence neighbors ... The friends that you can count on to pitch in on days that the kids are driving you crazy or you need help with childcare or pickups. They allow you a needed pause from the rat race of child raising and offer a helping hand when you need it. These people may not actually live next door but they may be the parents you know from the bleachers, PTA, or your child's classroom. When you have a few friends who can pick your child up from school when they are sick and you are stuck at work then you know that you are blessed. They are dependable and reliable. The challenge for you is to reciprocate the service. Are you that kind of friend for your neighbors?

Your kindred spirits ... These are friends who share common interests, values, and goals. They are the people in your life that you play with, lunch with and talk to. They feed your soul and you find that you feel better when you are in their presence. Conversation is an easy volley and they lift you up when you need it. These are the people who make life worth living and allow your world to be constantly expanding. Too often people think that their spouse should fill this need but having someone outside of your marriage to help you develop a sense of who you are allows the marriage to not suffer from the strain of too high an expectation. Your spouse is vital for some aspects of your life but friends serve to help you feel complete on a different level. This is especially true for woman who need to feel connected to other people for their well being. They are relational and therefore need to have relationships that are a bit varied for their different needs. Be cautious though of the friends who drain you and make you feel worse about yourself. Sometimes it is the up-beat complainer that can quickly rob you of your peace and make you feel worse after you are with them. Be on guard of those that may be needy and draining especially if you have a houseful of people that need tending to. They can rob the joy from you when you need it to tend to your immediate family. You don't have to sever these friendships but you should limit them and be wise on what they are doing to you. I found that if I spent time with someone like this I became short tempered and irritable with my own family. The lack of peace I felt when I was with them robbed me of much needed strength that I needed to run my home. I became wiser and the result was fewer but more important friendships.

Church family ... Too many people neglect this chapter of their child's life. They think they are too busy to attend church or they anticipate a battle to go to church. Developing an early habit of attending church allows your child an expectation that this is what we do on Sundays. Think about every time you get into a car and your children know that they must be in their carseat or have a seatbelt on. Since you started this practice the day you drove them home from the hospital there is an expectation that this is just what we do. The same will be true if you develop a habit of attending worship. The goal is the same, to keep them safe. Just as a seatbelt keeps your child safe so too will attending church allow your child to be safe. It is a dangerous world out there and all of the members of your family need the support that comes from having a spiritual home. It is comforting to have people lift you in prayer and supporting you if you have a need. There is comfort, especially in todays fast-paced lifestyle, to have rituals and traditions that calm us down a bit. To have a chance to be in fellowship with those who are on this journey beside you. To pause from the rat race and spend some quiet time in your Father's house. For your children, it allows them to get to know who their heavenly Father is and a chance to know his book, the Bible. During Confirmation they have an opportunity to have other mentors who help them affirm what was promised at Baptism, to be raised in the ways of the church and cultivate their faith. Many times they shut their parents out during this chapter of their life but to have adults, who have your child's best interest at heart, and mentor them is a real blessing. It also offers ministry opportunities for your child and that helps them see the world beyond themselves. They learn to feel safe with other kids who they share the program with and they develop a bond that may be present their entire life. The other aspect of a church community is the blessing of encounters with all different ages groups. With families spread all over the world it is important for children to know people from different stages of life. They can help hold the door for an 80 year old widow, see the generosity of people supporting a need to raise money for a missionary trip, or help with a mom whose hands are full with a two year old and a newborn. They get to raise their voice in song and recite prayers. They get to hide God's word in their hearts and that will serve them well throughout their journey.

School ... Understanding the importance of having a good relationship with your child's school and teachers helps to present a united front for your child's education. Open lines of communication allows your team to navigate the sometimes frustrating chapters of their schooling. Be involved with their education, know their teachers, get to know the students that they are sharing the journey with. Volunteer when possible and pay attention to the work that is coming home. If there is a conflict, be part of the solution not part of the problem. Be an advocate for your child but not an adversary to their school. Your child spends an awful lot of time at school and there are many pressures that they will feel from peer pressures to the burden of schoolwork. It is important that your child feels safe coming to you with any problems that they are experiencing so you don't want to overreact. From experience, I have also learned to get all of the facts first, as there was usually two sides to the story. After making some mistakes in this department, I finally learned to not just take my child's word for what happened but to become a fact finder and see if I could get to the bottom of what was happening. I realized that many times the situation wasn't exactly what was presented, so my job was to gain wisdom into the situation. Taking that approach allowed me to be calmer and help the situation instead of making thing worse.

Grandparents ... The value of having grandparents in your child's life is priceless. They offer support, patience, and a link to your child's history. They can be invaluable when you need help with childcare, or when your child is sick and you can't take off of work. Grandparents also typically enjoy being needed at this chapter of their lives. Their world is changing and between retirement and friends moving away they may have a limited exposure to the social world that they once knew. They are no longer active in their children's schools and activities and that allows them some free time to assist with your children. The most important aspect of this support system is to be sure that communication is occurring. When I teach the grand-parenting class I often tell the new grand parents to be cautious that they don't overstep their boundaries but also don't get taken advantage of. It is wonderful for them to be involved in the next generation but they have already raised their children so it is important to be sure that this chapter is balanced. Many grandparents are discovering that not only do they need to be supportive to their kids but their aging parents are in need of their help as well. This can quickly lead to burnout and that doesn't help anyone. Developing a good line of communication and a very clear understanding of the boundaries will help make this support system beneficial for everyone involved.

Coaches ... When your child begins to enter the world of sports and extra-curricular activities, other mentors are going to be part their lives. There was a study once that asked people who were the top in their fields; whether it was in a sport, music, or a skill; what was the one thing that you attribute to your success. Overwhelmingly, it was that their first exposure was fun. That their coach or music teacher made what they were doing enjoyable. As they grew in their skill level they wanted someone who would push them but initially they needed to learn to love it. When you watch Olympians give up their youth for their sport you know that they have an inner drive that came from a deep love of what they were doing. A gifted mathematician had someone who brought ease and clarity to their gift. Someone with a musical ear had a mentor who cultivated that passion. As you learn to be a student of your child you will start to see their natural gifts and with that you need to be constantly asking yourself how do you cultivate those gifts. I watched countless parents push their children to be on traveling teams, and sign them up for the elite programs to help them to be successful but in the end they became burned out and then by the time they enter high school and were on a major stage they gave up the sport. They were burnt out by the time they got to high school when they really needed a passion to keep them on track. I have also seen many a child underperform in grammar school, only to become the star in high school. They developed a fire in their belly that pushed them or their coordination finally kicked in that allowed them to excel at the sport. What I am saying is to look with open eyes at the programs that you sign your children up for. Are you doing it for your child or your own ego? My husband often says that he learned more from playing sandlot ball than he ever did from being on an organized team and he had more fun.

Coaches serve a valuable part of your child's life and their self-esteem. There are some outstanding coaches and unfortunately, some not so good ones. I challenge you to try to be supportive to whoever your child has, short of them being abusive, and be a team player as a parent. Your child is watching you and seeing how you handle yourself, so be a good role model. Everything we do is a learning experience and many times your child will learn more in the defeats and challenges than they ever will in the victories. When you watch your child involved in an activity, remember that the goal isn't always just the win but in the learning experience. Watch to see if your child is a good sport, do they encourage others or are they too absorbed in their own performance that they don't see beyond themselves? Are they respectful to the coach? Are you? How do you speak of the coach at the dinner table? Always remember that your child is watching. This is a time of learning and the goal is to expand your child's world and teach them a skill. The trophies will likely end up in the attic, but the character that they learn will last them a lifetime. My four kids were involved in sports and the proudest moment for me as a parent was that all four of them won the sportsmanship award in high school. It was an award given to the teammate who showed good sportsmanship both on and off the field. That is a life goal!

There will be other team members on this journey of raising your child such as their first boss, a babysitter, your next door neighbors, their close friends, etc. Each experience is teaching your child something and your goal is to watch with open eyes to see what they are learning.

Third ... be the great encourager. Be the cheerleader for your child. Be wise enough to know what your team is capable of doing and what they can't do. If dad was the outstanding athlete in school but his son has all left feet, look for what strengths he does have. Don't let your dreams become your child's, let them have their own dreams and passions. Now that I am a grandmother, I can no longer roll tack the boat (heeling the boat far to one side and then heeling it far to the other side when you go through a tack), as a matter of fact I am just thrilled when I can make it across the boat without falling down. My skipper (my husband) understood my limitations and was just thrilled to have me in the boat. What I lacked in agility I made upon for in knowledge (and a comfort of having the team together). Our expectations changed but after over 40 years sailing together we still have fun. Would your kids say that you are an encourager? Would they say that living in your home is fun? Would they say that they could count on you when the chips are down? All important questions to ask and discuss. It's never too late to change the tone of your home. You are not always going to be perfect at this parenting job but is the overall tone in your home positive and upbeat. Do the family members feel safe? Do you? Begin today to enhance and strengthen the tone in your home so that everyone can thrive. Call out to the biggest cheerleader of all ... God. He will encourage, love, strengthen and support you when you need it. He even wrote a book about it.

Forth ... Evaluation of Character. You won't win every race. How do you handle the setbacks , the breakdowns, the missed opportunities. Sometimes you just can't see the wind shifts or you had a screwup at a mark rounding. How does your team handle the disappointments? What type of character does your team have? As you gain wisdom as a parent you are able to learn how to assess your child's character and see how they are progressing. Understanding character traits lets you be on the lookout for both the positive and negative traits that you see in your family (it also helps you see your own growth).

Trials will come and so will disappointments. That is life. But how you handle these setbacks will show your character.

7 positive traits are:
Honesty ... Can you trust what they say or do?
Bravery ... Do they stand tall when the storms come and move to action?
Compassion ... Do they show kindness and comfort to those in need?
Unselfish ... Do they share of themselves and their gifts?
Loyal ... Do they show loyalty to the family and their friends?
Content ... Do they like who they are?
Respectful ... Do they value the people they share this life journey with?

The goal is to do periodic evaluations of the family so that you can assess where everybody is. If you see character traits going the wrong way then it is important to make your child aware of it so that they can change.

The following is a chart where you can evaluate your child and do an inventory on their character. It can help you assess if they are nice, mean or sad.

NICE	MEAN	SAD
Peaceful	Rude	Lonely
Respectful	Thoughtless	Moody

Friendly	Hateful	Heartbroken
Sensitive	Uncaring	Sorrowful
Sweet	Unfriendly	Unhappy
Thoughtful	Unpleasant	Withdrawn
Caring	Cruel	Depressed
Kind	Impolite	Heavy-hearted

This chart helps you to identify personality traits:

Active	Bored
Mature	Immature
Patient	Impatient
Trustworthy	Untrustworthy
Assertive	Anxious
Certain	Fearful
Independent	Uncertain
Responsible	Irresponsible
Fair	Unfair
Confident	Nervous
Gentle	Rough
Busy	Neglectful
Hard-working	Uninterested
Ambitious	Indifferent
Energetic	Sluggish
Funny	Serious
Quiet	Noisy
Leader	Follower
Calm	Reactive

By paying attention to the character of the people that you live with, you can see if minor tweaks need to be made or if they are progressing toward a major character flaw. Remember, you can't change people but you can educate them and you can educate yourself.

Perhaps you see a sour teenager and they see themselves as navigating a battle.

Fifth ... Make it fun. There is enough stress out there that you want to try to keep it out of your home. Too much drama can cause restless nights, yelling, short tempers, and anxiety.

Who wants that in your home? Begin today to rid your home of negative emotions. Clean house! Don't allow disrespect to run free in your home. Cursing shouldn't be allowed, it shows an immaturity anyway, and the goal is to help everyone to become more mature.

Yelling shows a lack of self-control (one of the Fruits of the Spirit) and disrespect is more a reflection on yourself than anyone else. Try today to change the tone and make your home one that everyone craves to be at. A place where the members feel safe and valued. Where people greet you when you come home at the end of a long day and where people know how to laugh. Life is too short and fleeting to not have some fun along the way. Bring it into your home in big doses. It doesn't require money or a whole lot of time. It means that the mood is light enough that its members can laugh at themselves and others and that they can laugh with each other. They enjoy mealtime and those precious moments when no one has to be anywhere else but home. Cherish those moments.

CHAPTER 8
The Value Of The Compass

~·~

The compass may be the most valuable piece of equipment that you carry if the weather conditions change. If a fog bank rolls in and the shoreline is masked by the thickening clouds, a compass may be the only sight that you have. You may travel the same waterway for years and yet when the fog rolls in the coastline looks like a completely new place. The landmarks that were once so familiar look out of place and you may find yourself against a shoreline that looks entirely new. A blanket of fog can alter our perceptions and cause our judgement to be flawed.

We once had a race committee member who experienced what life was like when you get enveloped in a cloud of fog and can't see three feet in front of you. He was in his 70's and he had spent his entire life at the lake. He set out from his home by boat to get to the yacht club for the day's races with a light mist of rain falling. That cloud cover quickly turned into fog and even though he has driven to the club a thousand times he was completely and totally lost. He couldn't tell one shore from the other. Familiar landmarks lost their value as everything seemed different. He actually didn't know if he was heading north or south and a panic started to develop in him. He didn't have a compass in his motorboat so that reliable tool wasn't available and he felt helpless. He called the yacht club and asked his fellow race committee members to sound a horn so he could see if he was close. By being still and listening he was able to slowly and with great care find his way to the club. Left on his own he was totally and completely lost.

That is an example of our life without God. Yes, we can navigate fairly well on our own for most of the journey but when the fog of illness, a crumbling marriage, or a death in the family occurs our only hope may be in the promise of guidance by our compass.

When we can't see where we are or where to take the next step, God can slowly and steadily guide us in the proper direction forward. The challenge is to make sure that you bring the compass with you daily, for you don't know when that fog bank will occur. Likewise, it is vital to never send your child out without their compass. That simple step may be their only hope when the pressures of life cloud their thought process and soon they can't see anything with clarity. Compound that with a self induced cloud of drugs on a young mind and they may find themselves totally and completely lost.

A compass can be a lifesaver, especially if you are sailing in open waters and need a compass point to direct you to the safety of the harbor. It can lead you home. Before heading out into open water, we always try to know ahead of time the compass point that will lead to the inlet and the safety of the harbor. When you get away from the shoreline the landmarks get blurred and you can quickly loose a sense of where to point the boat for the journey home. The compass will let you know which direction to turn the boat.

A compass is also a valuable tool to have when you are racing. It can let you know if you are sailing in a **lift** or a **header**. When you sail in a race the first mark is directly upwind from the starting line. A sailboat cannot sail directly upwind so it needs to go at about a 45 degree angle back and forth to reach the first windward mark. That is called tacking. If the wind is steady and the boats are evenly matched all of the boats on the starting line should be at the first windward mark at about the same time. But the wind isn't usually steady and it constantly shifts. If that shift takes you closer to the mark it is called a lift. If it takes you way from the mark it is called a header. An attentive sailor will be constantly reading the wind and looking for a lift to get him to the mark in first place. One way to do that is to look at your angle on the shoreline ... are you pointing higher on the course or lower? You can use the shoreline as a guide but if you are sailing in open water where the shoreline is far away or there aren't any noticeable markers on the shore then you must rely on your compass headings to guide you.

God is a wonderful compass that helps you stay on track and guide you when you feel lost. He is a reliable asset when the fog rolls in and you can't see your way through a situation or know your way home. He tells you when you are drifting away from the mark or when you are on course.

Sometimes, God uses situations in your life to warn you that you are in a header. Anxiety is a great warning that you are going away from the mark. When you feel anxious, a wise person will stop and assess what is going wrong and where they lost their peace. They can then assess if it is best to make a change, or hang on as it's just a temporary header. If you allow God to be your compass in life, He will always point you in the right direction. The more familiar you are with your compass, the quicker you can react to the lifts and headers that you will experience on a daily basis. Is this a wise decision? Should I take this job? Are my kids doing okay? If you feel an unrest (or downright anxious) then perhaps you are on the wrong tack and it is time to listen to your compass to tell you which is the right direction. This is called seeking wisdom. The compass gives you the ability to see clearly, even though there may be fog all around you or the shoreline is far away. The compass is dependable and it allows you to trust the compass points to guide you out of trouble. When you can't rely on the clarity of your sight you can rely on the clarity of the compass (God).

Putting your life situations to prayer keeps you in tune with the constantly changing conditions around you. When you start to know yourself, and your family members, you can tell immediately when something is off. The more attune you are, the quicker you can react and ward off trouble. Sailing in a header can lead you away from the mark, and it certainly makes you have to sail a longer distance. I see parents all the time sailing in headers. They are too distracted to notice that their child is heading for trouble. They see their marriage drifting off course but don't respond to the situation. They are anxious all the time and wasting precious energy that could be better utilized in positive actions that takes them toward their goal.

It is important to look at the big picture and see where you may need to make a change. Many times it is a simple tack (or a tweak) that can readjust your journey and have you sailing back toward the mark. Other times it is wiser to stay on course and look for opportunities that may be further along the journey that makes the change wiser. Sometimes, just taking in information allows you to determine what is the best course of action. Maybe the header was momentary and your need to not make a change is the wiser decision. Decide today to be a wisdom seeker. To rely on your compass for direction, and to ask yourself before you say yes, "Is this a wise decision?"

Teaching someone how to use a compass isn't always easy but once they understand the dynamics of the compass it makes complete sense. To understand the compass you must first understand the compass points. The North, East, South, and West are the campus points that comprise a compass and makes a complete circle. They represent the numerical degree points on a compass. North is 0, East is 90 degrees off of that point, South is directly opposite of North at 180 degrees and West is directly opposite of East at 270. To complete the journey around the circle brings you to 360 degrees or back to zero or due North.

In life I like to think of the compass in terms of character points that can guide you and keep you on track.

NORTH ... INTEGRITY

Integrity is described as the quality of being honest and having strong moral principles; a moral uprightness. "He is known as being a man of integrity." Some of the synonyms are; honesty, honor, good character ethics, morals, principled, fairness, sincerity, truthfulness, trustworthiness.

It also means the state of being whole and undivided with synonyms of togetherness, solidarity and wholeness, soundness, strength and durability.

Could you use those words to describe your children? How about yourself? Wouldn't it be nice if when people thought of you and your family those words came to mind.

So how to you cultivate integrity in your home? How do you make it so that you see integrity every time you see your face in the mirror, your children in the morning, and your spouse at the end of the day? Practice!

You need to identify what integrity is and make a conscious effort to practice it on a daily basis. Do your kids watch you gossip when you are on the phone with your friends? Do they see you cheat on your taxes? They are watching you every day and noticing your actions and modeling those behaviors. If it is okay for you to speak ill of another then it must be okay. To be a person of integrity means that you are fair, that you are trustworthy and truthful. If you make a promise to your child and then don't keep your word, then you are untrustworthy.

If you are partial to one child over another, then you aren't fair.

I taught a lecture once to a group of teachers about their role as an educator. I explained that as a nurse I am a professional, meaning that I took an oath that I would care for all of my patients fairly and to the best of my ability. I am a nurse whether I am in a hospital or on a soccer field. I am called to render care if and when it is needed. Even though patients may be under stress and not always pleasant, being a professional, I don't have the luxury of not liking a patient or not giving my finest care. Likewise, a teacher is a professional and as such they don't have the luxury of not liking or doing the best for a student. As a parent, the noblest of professions, you are called to a higher standard. You have little eyes watching everything you say and do and they will take that observation and incorporate it into their lives until it becomes the fabric of their being.

What kind of model are you for your kids? What did your parents model? If you had the blessing of your parents being great role models, then take a moment and thank them, for they gave you a great foundation. But if you weren't fortunate enough to have had integrity modeled for you then you may need to take a good look at your life and see what you are modeling for your kids. Are you repeating the sins of your parents, or are you making positive steps to change the legacy of your home? Learn to let go of your past and start today to alter the future of your family. You can't change the past but you can decide if you want to take what was given to you and become bitter or better. The choice is yours and yours alone. It is very powerful to give a parent grace and forgive them for their weaknesses. Build your foundation on a new model of parenting that comes from letting God be your Heavenly Father. He longs for a relationship with you and longs to give you the strength to change your family history. Remember, you are an heir to the throne ... it's time for you to be the role model of that position.

EAST ... COMPASSION

Compassion is described as sympathetic pity and concern for the sufferings or misfortunes of others. Empathy, understanding care, brotherly love, tenderness, gentleness and mercy. It also includes the synonyms leniency, tolerance, consideration and kindness.

Compassion ... the ability to understand someones's pain and to treat them with mercy. God knows that this is tough, so Jesus gave us the Sermon on the Mount to help us understand what he calls us to do. How He wants us to behave and how He empowers us to develop His heart.

In **Matthew 5,** Jesus gives us a sermon to describe how to find God's kingdom here on earth. He does it in the form of eight Beatitudes. They go from a simple faith to an intimate relationship and wisdom of who God is. They are a progression. Before we can be comforted we must have the attitude that we are "willing" to be helped. Step by step we can move to a closer relationship with God and with that be empowered to take control of our life.

The **First** Beatitude states "Blessed are the poor in Spirit, for theirs is the Kingdom of Heaven." This is a cry to God that says "I need help ... I can't do it on my own." Poor in Spirit means to humble yourself (surrender your arrogance) and ask for help. It is a challenge to admit your weaknesses and ask for guidance. The Bible is full of stories of people who came to the realization that they needed help. God's Hall of Fame includes the prodigal son, David , the adulterer, Saul who became Paul, Simon who became Peter, and Mary Magdalene to just name a few. These were people who cried out "Oh God, be merciful to me a sinner!" They then went on to do great things. With God's help you can move mountains but first you need to kneel before Him and ask for His help. When you can't stand any longer it is time to get on your knees.

The **Second** Beatitude is a beautiful promise from God. "Blessed are those who mourn, for they shall be comforted." The promise isn't "believe in me and you won't experience pain" but, rather, "when you are going through pain I will be beside you." What a wonderful promise! To know that no matter what trials you are experiencing, your Heavenly Father is right beside you. That you can feel peace and God's presence even during the storm. The question is, will you call out to Him to receive His comfort?

The **Third** Beatitude states "Blessed are the meek for they shall inherit the earth." We don't always think of meekness as something to strive for but I challenge you to look at it from God's point of view. Can you maintain your self-control during the challenges of life. Are you in control of your emotions and able to look at situations with wisdom and understanding.

Lets break the word MEEK up:

M ... Mighty. Who is stronger the man who gives in to his rage and becomes physically and verbally abusive or the man who remains calm, composed and assured of his inner strength? Might is the ability to control your emotions and develop a sense of inner discipline.

E ... Emotionally Stable. This is the person who can control his emotions and is able to keep his negative emotions in check. They resist temptation and are honest and hard working. They may have their ups and downs but they understand their goals and they muster through adversities with control. They will inherit the earth.

E ... Educated. These are people who seek wisdom. They are willing to learn, to be corrected, and to develop an understanding of the situation. They are teachable just like the Apostles. Jesus didn't pick the scholars of His day to start His ministry. He picked teachable rough and tumbling men who were able to be taught, transformed and trained to achieve His purpose. God calls you as well. He wants to show the world who He is by your actions. He wants the world to know His Shalom by others seeing your peace. He wants your children to have a relationship with Him by them seeing your relationship with God.

K ... Kindness. Without kindness the mighty are ruthless, the emotionally stable are cold and hard, and the educated are arrogant. Without kindness you only have MEE! These people can be self-centered and only think of themselves. Are you kind enough to be sensitive, thoughtful, and unselfish? Do you think of others and show compassion?

If you can become truly MEEK then you'll come to the end of your life being loved and respected. Who could ask for more? You'll inherit the earth.

The **Forth** Beatitude says "Blessed are those who hunger and thirst after righteousness, for they shall be satisfied." Having a strong desire to do the right thing and to be content in all situations. Matt. 6:33 says "Seek first the kingdom of God and His righteousness and all these things will be given unto you." Seek first what God has for you and all the other things in your life will fall into place. It is a call to say "Lord, I want to do the right things." That means feeding your body with good food, feeding your spirit with His wisdom and feeding your life with positive goals. Being selective and having a desire to live a positive life will allow you to grow good fruit and you will be satisfied.

The **Fifth** Beatitude tells us "Blessed are the merciful, for they shall obtain mercy." Compassion... Treating others as you would want to be treated. If you want to be happy, treat others right. That can be a challenge if they don't treat you well, but a mature person is able to look past offenses and decide to take the high road and show mercy anyway. It doesn't mean that they should tolerate another's abuse or that they need to carry the burdens of abuse on their shoulders. They choose to let go of past offenses and not let bitterness rule their life. It is empowering to "let go" of past offenses and give that burden to God. It also means to be merciful to thyself. Highly critical people often suffer low self-esteem and they have trouble living with themselves. Those that show mercy are able to shine in the darkness for that shine comes from within. Adversity makes them stronger and they gain wisdom and are able to be gracious to others.

Beatitude **Six** is "Blessed are the pure in heart for they shall see God." So we went from admitting that you need God, to the promise of comfort, advancing to being a person who is mature, to someone seeking God, and then learning to be gracious to the faults of others. Now we are at the stage where we are able to see God if we keep the pathway clear. It's the idea of letting God flow through me and developing a relationship so strong that His presence is part of my being. Do you wish you had more faith? Then you need to develop a purer heart. God calls us to be His temple but just like Jesus chased out the money changers when they contaminated His Father's temple, so God desires to clean us up so that His Holy presence can dwell within us. This step is not so much a matter of being a Biblical scholar but it is a matter of transforming your heart. What makes us different from the animals that roam this earth is that we have a basic instinct to know God. Our whole being is longing for a Spiritual presence in our lives. Animals do not have that same instinct. Belief is normal, unbelief is abnormal. The only way that you can see God clearly is to clean up your act. Clean up the negative things that blocks your faith and keeps you from seeing God such as anxiety, worry, addiction, guilt and pressures. Once you make right with God you start to see Him in everyday happenings in your life. You then begin to have a faith that flows through you.

"Blessed are the peacemakers for they are called children of God" is the **Seventh** Beatitude. It calls us to be peacemakers. Did you ever meet someone who knew how to do that? They seemed at peace even when the world was in chaos around them. They are the people that know they are children of God. They possess a comfort and confidence of knowing that God is their Father, therefore they can rest assured that the battle has been fought and has already been won. They know they are on the winning team. They promote peaceful resolutions to any conflict because they are at peace themselves. They aren't weighed down with a lot of extra burdens because they don't carry extra emotional garbage around with them. They are lean and confident that God will provide and as a result they don't feel like victims. They strive to bring out the best in others because they feel like God brings out the best in them. They know their mission and that is to bring glory to God and on the day the journey is over they long to hear their Heavenly Father say "Well done my good and faithful servant".

The **last** Beatitude is really pretty remarkable. "Blessed are those who are persecuted for righteousness sake for theirs is the Kingdom of Heaven." This is one of the toughest lessons that simply stated means sometimes life just isn't fair! And if that is what I experience, I can make a choice to be happy anyway. If after applying all of the principals and positive attitudes that Jesus preached on the Sermon on the Mount to the best of my ability and I find myself the abused victim, I can choose to believe that God can settle the score in His own way and His own time. I can then "Let it Go" and move forward.

SOUTH ... FAITH

Faith is a tricky thing. It is a trust in something that we can not see. It is taking a step of faith when we don't know where that step will take you. It is letting go of our need to be in control and letting God take the wheel. It is something that you can't give to someone else but something that must be cultivated in our own lives. God has "Children of God" not grandchildren. We don't have faith just because our parents do, it is something that is unique to each one of us. God did an amazing thing when He put Adam and Eve on this planet. He gave them a "free will" that allowed them to choose whether they wanted a relationship with Him. He doesn't mandate that you believe, but He does proclaim that you have no excuse to not believe for all you have to do is look around at His creation to see His presence.

When I was changing from one church to another, I knew my father had concerns. He was the one who cultivated my faith and he was afraid that I may be turning my back on God. I will never forget what his words were to me. "Don't forget how important your faith was when your sister died, don't deprive your children of that." He basically was telling me that if I only get one thing right it is to till the soil of my children's faith. To help them know who God is and that this journey's ultimate goal is to bring you home. When I was caring for my dad in his final days on this earth his faith was rock solid. He wasn't afraid to die and was actually ready to experience it. He taught me many things during my lifetime but the one that will always stand out is that he taught me how to die. Many people know how to live well but it is a real challenge to die well. To die at peace and to have the bold confidence of knowing that you are almost home. My final gesture with my dad as he lay in a medically sedated state was to pray aloud with him. I recited the Our Father and The Lord is My Shepherd and I watched his mouth moved with the reciting of these prayers. He was present with the Lord and ready to be greeted by my sister who was only 20 years old when she made the heavenly journey home. That is real comfort!

Hiding God's words in your child's heart takes time. I play a Christian CD in the car when I am driving my grandkids and they sing the words at the top of their lungs. I tell them Bible stories like I did for their parents. I take them to church and try to model God's presence in my life. By tilling the soil of their faith it allows the seed to take root. The seed is very good but won't grow if the soil is hardened and not watered. My job is to till the soil and make sure it has sun and water to help it grow. It takes time for the seed to take root but I have faith and patience to watch it grow for I have the Master Gardener to talk to. He can guide me if I am giving it too much water or not enough. If the sun is drying it out or the shade is preventing it from blooming He advises me. He knows my plant and He asked me to take care of it for Him. My skills aren't good but I know that His are, so I just put my faith in Him. It worked well for my own four kids and I trust that it will work for my growing family.

The opposite of faith is anxiety. The feeling of distraction, choking, or strangulation. It is a painful uneasiness due to an impending fear. It is a mental, emotional, and spiritual strangulation. At its mildest, we churn inside; at its worst we panic.

Think of it this way ... the beginning of anxiety as the end of faith.

WEST ... RESPONSIBILITY

Responsibility, taking ownership for your own actions and not blaming someone else for your mistakes. Today we see a lot of people blaming others for their shortcomings. "I'm this way because my parents divorced." "I did this because my teacher made me mad." "I did this because no one understands me." No, you did this because you chose to do that. We are not victims who have no control over ourselves. As we grow in maturity and faith we can begin to see things with a clarity that we didn't see before. We shed the hurts and pains of our youth and decide to break free of the bonds that hold us hostage when we fail to forgive. We get tired of the ruts that keep us going in circles where we make the same mistakes over and over. It is time for us to get off of the pity pot and start taking control of our own lives. If you sit on that pot too long all you get is a sore behind. Take ownership of your life and realize that only you have control over your feelings and behaviors. The blame game is over and it is time to strive for maturity. Develop an attitude where you strive for understanding of the situations and people in your life.

I see people all the time make the same mistakes over and over and they don't seem to learn from their actions. Pretty soon they find themselves in a deep hole of debt, stress, or unhealthy relationships. They never seem to grow in a positive way and therefore find themselves in a deep dark hole. My attitude is that when you find yourself in a hole it is time to stop digging.

We want to shed our old ways of thinking and discover the freedom of living side by side with God. We can unload our burdens and ask Him to take our baggage. We can walk freer and with more confidence for we know that we are loved and that God has a plan for us. We are no longer walking aimlessly without direction. The path is clear but God tells us that it is narrow so we need to be on guard so that we don't lose our way or leave the well marked trail. When we experience anxiety (that gnawing feeling that something isn't right) we know that we have left the trail and that we need to call out to God to get us back on track.

We start to look to ourselves to fix things instead of God. We think that we are responsible for keeping the world spinning and we take our eyes off of the promises that God has given us. God wants our vision to be focused on Him and all the promises that He provides. The trouble with so many families these days is that they fail to trust God or don't have a clue what His promises are. Then it becomes impossible to pass God's wisdom on to the next generation. If the current generation is bankrupt on the peace and joy that God gives to all who believe, then trying to pass that on gets to be harder and harder.

In **Matthew 14:22-33** we are reminded of what it means to trust God. The story begins with Jesus sending the Apostles out onto the sea where they are to go to the other side. Jesus had just finished feeding the multitudes with five loaves of bread and two fishes that a small boy provided. They were able to feed the large crowd with plenty left over and then Jesus was able to heal the crowd both physically and spiritually. This left Jesus drained and needing to go off alone to spend some time with His heavenly Father in prayer while the Apostles were trying to make sense of the miracle they had just witnessed. As the Apostles crossed the sea without Jesus in their boat, a storm came up and the boat was tossed by the waves. When they looked up they saw Jesus walking on the water to greet the boat that Peter and some of the other Apostles were on. They were frightened and Jesus responded "Do not be afraid." Peter sees Jesus walking on the water and he is bold enough to think that he can walk on water as well. As long as his focus is on Jesus he is successful but as soon as he looks down at his own two feet, he becomes afraid and he begins to sink. Peter's cry is "Lord, save me!" Jesus immediately reaches out his hand for Peter and says, "Oh you of little faith, why do you doubt?" When Peter gets back in the boat the winds cease and the boat is calm. The Apostles were in awe. He wants us to do the same thing. To call out to God and let His hand take you out of your sinking despair. God is telling us that on your own you can be overwhelmed, but with God as your focus you can do anything.

Our kids need to have a compass that guides them on this journey they are on. They need to learn how to tell if they are traveling toward God or away from Him. Are they on the right path or are they traveling away from God's helping hand? A compass guides us but without it we can be lost. By knowing the direction they need to go they can follow that North Star to get them to the safety of home. Be reassured that God is fighting your battles, arranging things in your favor, and making a way even when you don't see a way. Put your compass in your boat and learn to trust what it says. The Bible is full of reassuring promises that we can trust.

> **Is. 41:10** Do not be afraid for I am with you. Do not be dismayed for I am your God. I will strengthen you and guide you.

Prov. 3:5-6 Trust in the Lord with all your heart and lean not on your own understanding; in all your ways acknowledge him, and he shall direct your paths.

Psalm 37:23 If the Lord delights in a man's way, remakes his steps firm; though he stumble, he will not fall, for the Lord upholds him with his hand.

Integrity is choosing your thoughts and actions based on values that lead to maturity, wisdom, and character. What are your compass points? Where are you and your family going? Begin today to do an assessment of your life and the direction that your family is traveling. It really isn't as hard as it may seem if you ask God to guide you and help you on this journey. Just as you need to learn how to use a compass and understand what it is telling you, you also need to learn who God is. The more you learn about God and what His direction is for you the easier it is for you to hear His voice. He will guide you and help you achieve wisdom in the decisions that you make for your family. The promise that He makes to us over and over again is that He will bring us His peace and I think we can all benefit from a bit more peace in our lives.

CHAPTER 9

Don't Leave Shore
Without Your Anchor

e have our lifejacket, and our compass. We have assembled
our team and taught our kids how to navigate their boat.
We are preparing them to set off from the safety of the shoreline and
venture into the open seas. But before we send them out on their
own there is another tool that will help them on their journey and
that is their anchor. An anchor is a device, normally made of metal,
used to connect a vessel to the bed of a body of water to prevent the
craft from drifting due to wind or current.

As it relates to a person, the word anchor means that the person
can be relied on to keep a project, an organization, or a family in
the right place. An individual is an "anchor" for another person by
providing stability and connectedness.

What is the purpose of an anchor and why don't you ever want
to leave the safety of the harbor without one? The value of an anchor
is that it can hold you steady when a storm hits or if you are in seas
with a strong current. An anchor rarely gets used when you are competing in a race, but it may be that last safety tool that you need to
prevent a dangerous situation from developing. In our fleet it is a
mandatory tool that must be in the boat or we will be disqualified
if we finish the race without one.

The storm ... One year we raced in Fort Walton Beach, Florida in August when thunder storms can spring up quickly due to the warm temperatures and unstable air masses. That happened one day as we were competing in the National Championship with close to 100 boats. Due to an impending storm the race committee cancelled the race and sent us in. The goal was to get the boats off the water before the storm hit but as we approached the safety of the harbor you could see the black sky up ahead and knew that danger was moments away. We immediately put on our lifejackets, took down our main sail and prepared the anchor. We were relying on our smaller jib sail to take us in but once the storm hit there would be no telling what we would be faced with. The roar of the storm was the first thing I remember, followed by a sheet of rain so strong and dark that you could barely see the boat next to you. The storm was loud and with the flapping of the sails it became nearly impossible to hear what the skipper was saying. It was vital that we knew what the plans were before the storm hit. Lifejackets on, main lowered, anchor ready. We knew the compass heading and now we just had to weather the storm. The jib kept us from being cast aimlessly about and the tiller, though hard to manage, allowed the rudder to guide our way. If we lost the sail or the rudder broke we would be in big trouble and that is when the anchor would be our only hope. By casting out the anchor we could hold our own and it would prevent us from being swept into the rocky shoreline or send us out to sea. It would be used to just hang on and wait out the storm.

God calls us to let Him be our anchor. To hold us still when the storms hit. It can prevent us from being cast about by whatever life brings our way. He challenges us to take Him along in our boat and to not leave the safety of the harbor without His presence.

Hebrews 6: 19 This hope we have as an anchor of the soul, both sure and steadfast.

What is the hope that is being referred to in Hebrews? It is the hope of eternal life, the promise of God's salvation and the reassurance of His Holy Spirit beside you on your earthly journey. The anchor of our soul is steadfast when we trust God's promises and call out to Him.

> **Jer 29:11** For I know the plans I have for you declares the Lord, plans to prosper you and not harm you. Plans to give you hope and a future.

Hope ... trusting something to be true. Hope is certain; it is an anchor of the soul both sure and steadfast. According to the Bible, Christ is "our hope" (1 Tim 1:1) and our God is called "The God of hope" (Rom 15:13). Hope is an understanding that we are on a pilgrimage to a destination called heaven and eternal life. We are called to a level of preparedness since we should be ready to leave this world at any time. (2 Cor 5:6-8) Hope calls us to be patient (Rom 8:25) Hope gives us strength and confidence for running the race and fighting the good fight. (Rom 8: 18). Our hope is our anchor that provides a firm foundation and security. It represents God and faith and a confidence in knowing that it will hold us in place no matter what storms we encounter.

Your children will be heading out into some pretty dangerous storms and the weather conditions in their life can change in a moment's notice. They need to be prepared and know what to do when those times come. Once the storm hits they may not be able to see or hear and so they must rely on the tools they have in their boat.

When my kids were younger I tried to hide God's word in their hearts. The promises that He gives them that they aren't alone, that He loves them, and that He hears them when they call out to Him. The promises that He makes are for each and everyone of us, yet if we don't know them we can't use them as our anchors to hold us still in the storms.

> **Psalm 16:8** *I have set the Lord before me; because he is at my right hand, I shall not be shaken.*

The comfort of knowing that we have an anchor beside us, allows us to weather the storm with confidence. It can still be scary but by trusting our anchor to hold us steady we can just hang on and ride it out.

The other times when an anchor is needed is when the winds die and you are in a body of water that has a strong current. Sailing in a regatta on the Delaware River proves challenging but especially so when the winds die and the current threatens to carry you out toward the Atlantic Ocean. One day during a race we had to round a mark upriver but the wind died and the current was carrying us down river. We couldn't paddle or we would be disqualified. We watched as our mark was getting further and further away. Once we rounded the mark we could let the current carry us down stream to where we needed to go but until then we were at the mercy of the water flow. What did we do? We cast out our anchor. It held us in place as we waited for the breeze to fill back in. Some of the boats around us didn't do that and they drifted away from the mark and further and further behind. The anchor will hold us still as we wait for the breeze.

The scripture tells us to "Be still and know that I am God." **Psalm 46:10.**

There are times when forward motion isn't possible. We just need to sit and rest in the promise that He is God, He holds us in the palm of His hand and He wants us to rest in His presence.

Our kids need to hear that message. Their lives are so busy, and with so many pressures that they feel, sometimes the best thing that they can do is to drop anchor and rest. They need to know that resting is not only good but needed.

THE POTTER

To help us to know God's principles, the Bible is filled with word pictures that allowed the people to understand what He meant. The shepherd, the lost coin, and the prodigal son are some examples that are used throughout the Bible to bring meaning to God's lesson.

In Isaiah the prophet equates God to being the potter and we are the clay. The people at that time knew about pottery and understood the stages that were necessary to take a lump of clay and make it something useful for the potter's purpose.

A potter begins to form his piece using a hard block of clay. He uses water to slowly soften the clay until it is pliable and able to be molded into the vision of the creator. Without water it is nearly impossible to mold the clay into the desired shape. Slowly and lovingly it is molded by the refreshing water and warm hands of the potter into something useful. As the potter softens the piece he transfers the clay to the spinning wheel where it can be turned and shaped. When it is put on the potters wheel it is vital that it is centered so that it can be shaped properly. The clay is spinning and it gradually takes the shape that the potter desires. Once the potter is pleased with the piece he lets it "rest." If the clay is handled too soon the piece will collapse and it will be worthless. The clay needs to develop some hardness so that it can withstand being manhandled.

The promise that God gives us in Isaiah is that He is our potter and we are the clay. He has a desire to mold us into something that is useful.

Isaiah 64:8
But now, O LORD, You are our Father, We are the clay, and You our potter; And all of us are the work of Your hand.

God tells us that He has important work for us to do. He wants us to become a vessel that can be useful and He wants us to cultivate that same message to our children. He shapes us, molds us, and desires for us to be a glorious vessel that is useful for His purpose. We are each unique and serve different purposes just as each of the potter's pieces are all unique. Some pieces have extra adornments such as handles or decorations that need to be added and others are very functional and simplistic but still serve a purpose. The potter will assess each piece once it is hardened to determine if clay needs to be added or removed to achieve his desire for the piece. Sharp tools will be used to shape, add, or remove clay. Sharp incisions may be used to cut off anything that hinders its usefulness. The potter may use a scalpel to cut off extra baggage that the piece has or to graft extra clay to make a handle or decorative additions.

Sometimes life is like that. We may have to bear the pain of going through the process of having things in our life that are burdensome cut away so that they don't hinder what God has planned for us. Let's say we gossip and then we are called on it ... it isn't pleasant but the pain may be needed to help us correct the problem. A plant sometimes needs pruning to keep it healthy since the unhealthy branch is draining the plant and isn't contributing to its well-being. By pruning the draining branch you contribute to the health of the whole plant. By teaching your child that challenges and hurts are part of life, you allow them to be a healthier person who is able to withstand the trials of life. When they learn that they are being shaped by a great potter they will see challenges as a chance for growth. They can learn that sometimes you need to just rest on the wheel (regroup and refresh) until they are strong enough to be handled by the world again. They will learn that there are times when you need to just put out your anchor and hang on and let God hold you firmly.

Once the pottery has firmed up, it is ready to go into the fire. This is a real challenge but it is necessary to make it useful, otherwise it would be too porous and unable to hold anything. We will experience our own fires during our lifetime. Maybe an illness, or the loss of a loved one, maybe a job loss or an unexpected trial. All of them challenge us to become stronger. If a piece has flaws going into the fire, like an air bubble, the heat can cause it to shatter and damage the other pieces in the kiln. A potter will assess the pieces carefully before he puts them in the kiln. If he detects a flaw he will crush the clay piece and start the molding process all over again. He will never discard the clay but work to remake it without the flaw. Sometimes people need to hit rock bottom before they are able to be reworked into a useful vessel. It sounds tragic but when you see it from God's point of view it is actually quite loving. He wants you and your children to be useful.

After the fire, the piece is strong and able to stand on its own. It can be handled but the potter isn't done yet. He coats the piece with a glaze and after a second firing it comes out of the kiln reflecting the image of the potter. The glaze that our loving father coats us with is the Holy Spirit and now we carry a bit of His presence in us on a daily basis. What a beautiful image. We are now useful and able to serve His purpose. We reflect the image of the potter. We may even be called on to serve His purpose and pour his water on others to soften their clay.

The challenge for us is to understand that there are times when we must just rest in His presence. To allow His anchor to just hold us in place and wait for the storm to pass. To allow ourselves time to firm up so we can be taken from the spinning wheel.

I use to tell my children that when they get hit with a setback, it might just be God warning them. He is trying to get their attention. Sometimes that warning comes in the way of being hit with a pebble, a slight annoyance that gets your attention but doesn't block your way. But if we don't listen then it may be a rock that we experience that will certainly cause us to pause and think about what just happened. Unfortunately, sometimes it's a boulder that gets in our way and causes us to stop and hear God's voice.

My son was stopped once for speeding early one morning on his way to school. He was given a pass by the police officer and told to slow down. He understood that according to our rules if he got a ticket he would be responsible to pay for his car insurance for the year so I'm sure he had some concerns about the situation. Unfortunately, his concerns didn't even last a week as he got pulled over again for going too fast. This time he got a ticket and now was responsible to pay for both the ticket and his car insurance for that year. He didn't listen the first time when the pebble hit him (a warning), so he got hit again but this time it came in the form of a big rock (a ticket, financial obligations, and extra restrictions). We told him that the next time it could be more severe (a boulder) in the way of an accident where he might have been hurt or he might have hurt someone else. Listen and learn the first time and then God doesn't have to shout.

The Titanic was warned six times to "slow down," "change course," or "stop" due to the ice field in their path. Six times they could have changed the outcome of their journey but they didn't take heed. The consequences were disastrous and yet a simple heeding of the warnings could have changed the outcomes. God wants us to hear Him and listen to that small voice that guides us. He wants to be our anchor so that we don't drift away from him or crash upon the rocky shoreline.

By hiding God's promises in your child's heart, and your heart for that matter, you provide a sure and steady anchor in times of need. It will hold them strong when the storms of the world are around them.

Memorize scripture so you and your child will be able to pull it out at a moments notice to hold you steady. I used to challenge my kids to learn scripture by buying them whatever cereal they wanted if they could give me ten Bible verses. It was a simple and fun way to hide God's word in their hearts. I played children's Bible music in the car and studied the Bible with them. My goal was to enlighten them to God's promises and to educate me as well. The result that I achieved was that I was calmer and I feel like they were as well.

When my dad was dying and I was caring for him I used to recite the 23rd Psalm with him. The promise of the Good Shepherd taking care of his flock brought a great deal of comfort to my dad and I was glad that I had hidden God's blessing in my heart so that I could daily share it with my dad. I memorized that Psalm with my children never realizing that it would one day bring such comfort to someone I loved.

Hide God's word in your children's hearts so that when they need an anchor it will be close at hand. A word of caution; don't be surprised if your kids learn the verses quicker than you do, for they always outdid me in their memory verses. Maybe my mind was a bit too cluttered or maybe they were just a bit closer to God and they heard His voice clearer than I did.

BIBLE VERSES TO KNOW

To help you begin the journey of studying God's words and promises I have a few key Bible verses that you can begin to memorize.

Isaiah 40:28 *Do you not know? Have you not heard? The Lord is the everlasting God, the Creator of the ends of the earth. He will not grow tired or weary, and his understanding no one can fathom.*

John 3:16-17 *For God so loved the world that He gave His one and only Son, that whoever believes in Him shall not perish but have eternal life. For God did not send His Son into the world to condemn the world, but to save the world through Him.*

Romans 6:23
For the wages of sin is death, but the gift of God is eternal life in Christ Jesus our Lord.

Revelation 3:20
Here I am! I stand at the door and knock. If anyone hears my voice and opens the door, I will come in and eat with him, and he with me.

John 14:6
Jesus answered, "I am the way and the truth and the life. No one comes to the father except through me."

Ephesians 2:8-9
*For it is by grace, through faith, that you have been saved —
and this not from yourselves, it is the gift of God—not by works,
so that no one can boast.*

2 Corinthians 5:17
*Therefore, if anyone is in Christ he is a new creation; the old
has gone, the new has come!*

Romans 8:38-39
*For I am convinced that neither death nor life, neither angels
nor demons, neither the present nor the future, nor any powers,
neither height nor depth, nor anything else in all creation, will
be able to separate us from the love of God that is in Christ
Jesus our Lord.*

Matthew 11:28-30
*Come to me, all you who are weary and burdened, and I will
give you rest. Take my yoke upon you and learn from me, for I
am gentle and humble in heart ,and you will find rest for your
souls. For my yoke is easy and my burden is light.*

Psalm 27:1
*The Lord is my light and my salvation—whom shall I fear? The
Lord is the stronghold of my life—of whom shall I be afraid?*

Jeremiah 29:11
*"For I know the plans I have for you," declares the Lord, "plans
to prosper you and not to harm you, plans to give you hope
and a future."*

Isaiah 40:30-31
*Even youths grow tired and weary, and young men stumble
and fall; but those who hope in the Lord will renew their*

strength. They will soar on wings like eagles; they will run and not grow weary, they will walk and not be faint.

Proverbs 3:5-6
Trust in the Lord with all your heart and lean not on your own understanding; in all your ways acknowledge him, and he will make your paths straight.

Philippians 4:13
I can do all things through Christ who strengthens me.

Galatians 2:20
I have been crucified with Christ and I no longer live, but Christ lives in me. The life I live in the body, I live by faith in the Son of God, who loved me and gave himself for me.

James 1:22
Do not merely listen to the word, and so deceive yourselves. Do what it says.

Colossians 3:23
Whatever you do, work at it with all your heart, as working for the Lord, not for men.

Galatians 5:22-23
But the fruit of the Spirit is love, joy, peace, patience, kindness, goodness, faithfulness, gentleness and self-control.

Hebrews 12:1-2
Therefore, since we are surrounded by such a great cloud of witnesses, let us throw off everything that hinders and the sin that so easily entangles, and let us run with perseverance the race marked out for us. Let us fix our eyes on Jesus, the author and perfecter of our faith, who for the joy set before

Him endured the cross, scorning its shame, and sat down at the right hand of the throne of God.

Philippians 4:6,7

Do not be anxious about anything, but in everything, by prayer and petition, with thanksgiving, present your requests to God. And the peace of God, which transcends all understanding, will guard your hearts and your minds in Christ Jesus.

Psalm 23

The LORD is my shepherd, I shall not be in want. He makes me lie down in green pastures, he leads me beside quiet waters, he restores my soul. He guides me in paths of righteousness for his name's sake.
Even though I walk through the valley of the shadow of death,
[1] I will fear no evil, for you are with me; your rod and your staff, they comfort me.
You prepare a table before me in the presence of my enemies. You anoint my head with oil; my cup overflows.
Surely goodness and love will follow me all the days of my life, and I will dwell in the house of the LORD forever.

CHAPTER 10
When To Bellow

A lighthouse is a valuable safety feature on the shoreline throughout the world. It prevents many a disaster from occurring by it's very presence of a beaconing light. Back in the day many of these lighthouses were manned by a single lighthouse keeper who kept watch to spot a ship that may be in need. He was diligent to be sure that he had enough fuel to keep the light shining and faithful in looking out into the open seas, always searching for that boat that may appear on the horizon. The lighthouse was used as a marker for the boats that sailed during the day or when the skies were clear and the skipper could see the shoreline. But during the dark of night, an impending storm, or the blanket of fog it was invaluable to have a light powerful enough to penetrate the darkness. To be a beacon that could guide the vessel away from the dangers of the shore and to help them to navigate into a safe harbor. But sometimes even the powerful light was difficult to see if the storm was fierce enough to blind the light from view or if the fog was so thick that visibility was almost nonexistent. It was then that the mournful wail of the bellowing horn heard in the dark of night could be all that kept the boat from disaster.

As a parent it is vital to keep our light shining and keep ourselves refreshed so that we have enough fuel to ride out the storm. This preparation must be done before the storm hits when the days are lazy and we have time to refresh ourselves in God's word, surround ourselves with true friends who encourage and refresh us, and to cultivate our own gifts so that we feel empowered when we are called to duty. When the weather turns sour it is time to do what we have been preparing for and that is to power our light.

But what happens when the light isn't enough? It is time to "bellow!" A bellow is a heartfelt cry to the darkened sky ... a call for help. The journey is tough but God promised us over and over again that we are not on this journey alone. As a matter of fact we are told 365 times in the Bible to "Fear not," "Do not be afraid," "Do not be anxious."

Philippians 4:6-7.

6 Do not be anxious about anything, but in every situation, by prayer and petition, with thanksgiving, present your requests to God. 7 And the peace of God, which transcends all understanding, will guard your hearts and your minds in Christ Jesus.

"Be anxious for nothing" ... What is God telling us? He is teaching us how to bellow. How to cry out to Him when our world is dark or we are in the midsts of a storm. He tells us to **"bellow"** and call out to Him with prayer and petition. He then reassures us what the outcome will be ... PEACE!

When we pray we can follow a simple format or rely on memorized prayers. We can stand or get down on our knees, you can find a quiet spot in your home or go for a walk. But begin today to have what will hopefully be a lifetime of talking personally to God.

There is nothing wrong with reciting a rote prayer and, as a matter of fact, Jesus taught us the greatest prayer we have: "The Our Father." He was telling us that we have a Father that we can depend on and look to just as a hurting child can run to a loving father for help and guidance. We are being taught in that simple prayer that God wants a relationship with us. He isn't saying that He wants us to refer to Him as King and we are His subjects, but that we are His children and He is our father. What a blessing that is! We are heirs to the throne and as heirs we can call Him when we have a need or a problem. His promise is that we have a home waiting for us in heaven. But right now we are still on the journey and while we are traveling, we have the promise of a shining light that will guide us along the path.

Another way to pray is to remember the word ACTS. It is a more personal approach to talking with God. God wants us to get real and talk to Him heart to heart. Sometimes we forget that He already knows all that we are going through. He knows us better than we know ourselves, so nothing you can say or do will surprise Him. He knows that there are times that we blow it and don't handle things well. He is aware that maybe we are causing some of our own grief by our behavior and have failed to admit those short-coming to ourselves.

If you look back on the story of Adam and Eve in Genesis chapter 3 you can see that hiding from God is useless. When they ate from the tree of knowledge they tried to hide because of the shame they felt. God already knew what they had done but He was waiting for them to admit it. He was waiting for them to "bellow!"

God is okay with your bellowing. The parable in Luke chapter 18 tell of a widow who badgers the unjust judge until he gives in to her pleas. Jesus responds that His Father is a just judge that will hear your cries if you call out to Him.

So what does ACTS mean? It is a simple way for you to talk to God and cry out to Him in need.

A–Adoration
C–Confession
T–Thanksgiving
S–Supplication

ADORATION

First we acknowledge God as our Lord and Savior, as Our Father, as Our Creator. We stand in awe and praise His name. "Oh my heavenly Father..."

When you think about having a relationship with God it helps to understand who He is and what He wants from us. He gave us the 10 Commandments to help us on this journey to let us know when we get off track of His fellowship. (Exodus 20) Realize that the first three Commandments have to do with our relationship with our heavenly Father, our Creator.

I. I am the Lord your God, you shall have no other God before me.

God wants you to discover the still small voice within you and decide today to let Him be your Father. Deciding what you believe about God and how to practice your spiritually is a lifelong process of questioning and discovering. The Bible tells us that God wants a relationship with you and He wants you to be His child. He wants you to feel His presence and He wants you to call out to Him when you are hurting just as a little child will call out to a loving parent when they are in need. When He says I want you in My family, how will you answer? Exodus 20 tells us with the Commandments that He wants to partner with you to repair a broken world. Whether you are a strong believer, a strong nonbeliever, or somewhere in between, Exodus 20 presents quite a challenge. There is something intriguing and appealing about the idea of a small voice beckoning us to help complete the creation of the world by joining with God to repair it.

Our Heavenly Father gave us a choice and the choice is really very simple. We can choose today to be adopted into God's family and get all the benefits that come with being part of that family or we can choose to take this journey on our own.

He gave us a free will to make this choice. What will you decide? You can't make the decision for your children; you can certainly cultivate their faith but you can't give them faith, that is the choice that they need to make on their own. Their faith is something that they will need to choose for themselves. But if we don't cultivate their faith and plant in their hearts spiritual wisdom then they won't have the tools to make a wise decision. I think many times parents are afraid that they don't know enough about God to share who He is with them. As a result you will have two generations of weary travelers lost on their journey. How can you change that? Study who God is together. There are many resources out there to help you, all you do is have to be willing to try.

In the first Commandment God is telling us that He doesn't want anything to be worshiped above Him. Not fame, money, or possessions. He wants to be first in your life as you cannot serve two masters.

Matthew 6:19-34 challenges us to see where your treasures lie for that is where your heart will be. He challenges us to not store up our treasures on earth and forget about our treasures in heaven. He challenges us to not worry, but to trust Him and for us to be a light for others to see.

How do you develop this relationship?

1. Spend time with Him ... learn to hear His voice.
2. Pray ... talk to Him.
3. Be Quiet ... find time for quiet moments for the Lord speaks softly and the world is loud.
4. Know who He is ... read your Bible.
5. Learn the way home ... learn how to navigate the mountains and valleys in your life.
6. Put God first ... don't allow other idols (money, work, fame, pride, etc.) take a place above God.
7. God is always seeking the best for you but He also wants the best from you. He wants the "first fruits" of your labor and that is your time.

II. Do not take the name of the Lord your God in vain.

God wants and deserves you to treat Him with Honor and Respect. It is important to treat your family with Honor and Respect as we spoke about earlier, but it must start here with your creator.

How do you begin to be respectful and honoring to those we love? It starts with our tongue. In the book of James 3:1-12 we are taught about the power that the tongue has. Just as a small rudder steers a mighty ship or a bit can manage a horse so too should we manage our tongue. I see home after home abuse the power of the tongue. Parents talk disrespectfully to their child and then they wonder why their child is disrespectful. A spouse will curse at their partner and wonder why there is no respect in the home. If disrespect is common in your home call a family conference and start today to bring honor and respect back into your house. This is vital to a healthy home. You may have grown up in a home where disrespect was common, but begin today to change the legacy of your family. It is a challenge to change the course of a ship but with the turn of the rudder you can slowly and steady make that change.

As I became a new bride and then a new mom I knew that I wanted a home of peace and calm. I prayed that I would have the peace inside me that I could share with my young family. I tried to never embarrass my children in front of anyone and I have tried to never curse at my husband. It doesn't mean that we don't have arguments or that we don't have conflicts with our children but we maintain the attitude that we respect each other. That attitude starts first and foremost with respecting and honoring our God.

III. Remember the Sabbath day and keep it Holy.

How do you unwind each week from the stresses of life and find a way to reconnect with the people you care about? How do you set aside time to find inner peace? Why do some people have peace when their world is in turmoil and others can barely make it through the day? The answer is that "People need the Lord." We are born as spiritual beings who have an inner desire to reconnect with our Godly maker. But God gives us a free will and allows us to make the choice of cultivating that relationship. The way to know and love God is to spend time with Him. We sometimes look at the Sabbath as something that we "have to do" rather than we "get to do." The Sabbath means to "REST!" To refresh yourself. To spend some time meditating and resting in God's presence. Even God rested. The scripture tells us that both God and Jesus rested. After He created the earth "He rested."

God is saying that as your father, He wants you to respect Him, listen to Him, and talk to Him. He wants a relationship with you! You are His child and you are precious in His eyes. NOTHING you can do or have done will change His love for you. But when you wander away from Him, or do things that block His light you can get lost and end up crashing on the shoreline of life. When you feel lost, call out to Him, He listens!

The next Commandment is the only one with a promise attached to it.

4. Honor … Honor your Father and Mother and all will go well with you.

God gave us parents to act on His behalf. Honoring your parents anchors society and binds children to the community of faith. It helps us to know what love is. It is the link between our Heavenly Father and the people that we will be sharing our journey with. It is an intimate connection with someone who helped in the drama of creation and was called to nurture and care for you. It doesn't mean that you aways have to agree with your parents or completely understand their motives but we are called to honor them just as we are called to honor God. God gives us a commandment that calls us to honor His choice of a caregiver and as a result we will experience His peace and it will result in blessings in our life. Unfortunately, sometimes parents don't always provide us with an example of God's unconditional love and that is truly sad. If that is your model then I challenge you today to change the legacy of your family and don't let your kids say the same about you. "Bellow" and call out to God and ask for His help and wisdom to become the mother and father that you wished you had.

The rest of the commandments deal with our relationships with the people that we share the planet with. It is not always easy to deal with imperfect people when we ourselves are imperfect as well. We need to make a choice to treat people with kindness and grace. The Bible tells us that we have two choices; to be wise or foolish.

Matthew 7:24-27
The Wise and Foolish Builders
24 "Therefore everyone who hears these words of mine and puts them into practice is like a wise man who built his house on the rock. 25 The rain came down, the streams rose, and the winds blew and beat against that house; yet it did not fall, because it had its foundation on the rock. 26 But everyone who hears these words of mine and does not put them into practice is like a foolish man who built his house on sand. 27 The rain came down, the streams rose, and the winds blew and beat against that house, and it fell with a great crash."

Which will you choose? He wants you to have a firm foundation and a strong faith. He gives us foundational truths to build our lives. When the foundation is strong we can build on that and have stable relationships with the people around us.

The rest of the commandments basically tell us how to get along with this world full of imperfect people. After all, we are all imperfect people who may have married an imperfect person and have a house full of imperfect kids surrounded by a bunch of imperfect neighbors. Once you get this you can accept your assignment of just learning how to get along with this fishbowl of society.

V. **Thou shall not kill.** This not only addresses the physical action of murder but also killing someone's spirit, self-esteem, or value.

VI. **Thou shall not commit adultery.** The act of being faithful to the person you committed to share your journey with.

VII. **Thou shall not steal.** Not only someone's possessions, but robbing someone of their peace.

VIII. **Thou shall not bear false witness against your neighbors.** This refers to lying and misrepresenting people.

IX. **Thou shall not covet your neighbors house.**

X. **Thou shall not covet your neighbors goods.** These last two refer to a jealousy over what someone else has. Coveting robs you of your contentment and your peace.

What is the promise if you follow this blueprint for life? A journey that is "light-filled," the ability to experience peace during chaos, and the confidence of knowing that you have the key to your room in heaven.

"The greatest act of faith takes place when men finally decides that he is not God."

Johann Wolfgang von Goethe

CONFESSION

What extra weights are you carrying around? What burdens are weighing on you and making the journey harder? I once gave counsel to a young couple that was getting married and I knew from his background that the groom had parents who filled his backpack up with burdens that no child should have to carry. Normally loving parents try to shelter their kids from the burdens of life until they are stronger and able to carry those pressures. In this case he had spent his first 24 years carrying a backpack filled with his parents' insecurities and problems. Now he is trying to start his own family but weighed down with a backpack full of burdens that will hurt his future. When I told him to dump out his backpack and let go of the pressures he was carrying, it brought tears to his eyes. I challenged him to change the legacy of his family and the only way to do that is to let go of his burdens.

There is a challenge that you can try. Hold a glass of water out perpendicular to your body. Not hard right? But the longer you hold it out there the harder it becomes to keep your arm up. It slowly becomes unbearable and you long to put the glass down. God is telling you to put your glass down! To dump out your backpack! To let go of the burdens that are weighing you down. Give it to God and let Him carry your burdens. He longs to make your journey light and He wants you to turn your cares over to Him.

When you look back at the scripture that says, "Be anxious for nothing ..." He is saying that he wants you to talk to Him about what is bothering you. With prayer and petition (tell him what you want) make you requests known to God.

Confession will ease your burdens and allow you to let go of those things that are robbing you of your peace.

If you can't sleep at night, instead of counting sheep, talk to the shepherd. He is a good listener.

THANKSGIVING

"People travel to wonder at the heights of mountains, at the huge waves of the seas, at the vast compass of the ocean, and at the circular motion of the stars yet they pass themselves by without wondering who they are and what is their purpose."
Saint Augustine

Thanksgiving ... to be truly thankful for the blessings that we have. It is interesting how I have met people who have so little yet are more content than many who have a lot. What is their secret? What allows them to be at peace and generous when those with more resources are self-centered and restless? They have an intimate relationship with their heavenly Father and that brings them peace and contentment. We live in a world of "If only..." If only I had this I would be happy, if only my kids would behave I would be happy, if only my spouse made more money I would be happy. The list goes on and on.

The trouble with "If only ..." is that the person is always looking at what they don't have instead of what they do. If you only have God in your life you have everything!

When I teach my confirmation class I try to explain what it is like to have God in your life. I use the example of a parachute to explain the contrast of a life with God and one without. Having God in your life is like jumping out of a plane with a parachute on: you can enjoy the free fall because you trust the landing. Not having God in your life is like jumping out of the plane without a parachute. You can't enjoy the free fall because you're afraid of the landing. We all know people who are in a panic free fall and their life is always spinning out of control. They lack peace and joy because they are always worried. If this describes you, grab your parachute and start today to experience the joy and peace that comes from knowing God. And then you can start finding joy in the journey.

Enjoy the journey by opening your eyes and looking at the blessings around you. When you see and acknowledge your blessings it enables your kids to see them as well. My daughter taught her children this lesson by going around the table at dinnertime answering these questions.

What are you thankful for?
What were the best and worst parts of your day?
Who did you help today?
Who helped you today?

My daughter opened up her children's eyes to the blessings and opportunities around them. They will enviably grow up to be grateful people.

SUPPLICATION

Supplication ... to make your requests known. The action of asking or begging for something earnestly or humbly.

God challenges us to go ahead and list your requests or concerns. Call out to Him about what your needs are. Make a list of your prayers and concerns and turn them over to God. You'll be amazed that one by one they will start falling off your list as prayers are answered.

A warning ... Sometimes we think that just because we want something and ask God for it, the answer will be yes. That isn't the way a loving Father works. Just because a child wants candy before dinner doesn't mean a father will give it to him. It isn't the right time or maybe it isn't in the best interest for the child.

Sometimes God says yes, sometimes the answer is no and sometimes He says later "In His good time."

The promise is that He will answer you each and every time, in His time. The one thing that He will always give you is His peace, if you trust Him. When you learn to trust God and start to see the way He works you will be able to see that there is a reason for all He does. When you start to rely on God's timing you can relax and not fret and then you will begin to see His hand in your life.

Calling out to God and listing your concerns allows you to see the big picture of your problem. When my son was younger he was not attentive with his school work and homework was always a challenge. It was always a struggle at dinnertime to get his homework done without drama. I felt like I was a Charlie Brown parent, saying "wha, wha, wha," with no actual words being spoken or heard. Then one day, when I was tired of hearing myself talk, I turned it over to God. I sat down with my son and said that there would be a consequence for not doing his work but I wasn't going to nag anymore. I was there to help if he was struggling but I wasn't going to ride him like I did. If his homework wasn't done before practice, I took him to the field on time and he could sit in the bleachers and do his work until it was completed before he was allowed to practice with the team. I prayed constantly and let God handle the heavy lifting. Do you know what happened? He went off to college and pulled a 4.0 his first three marking periods. Today he is a middle school principal, and completed his Masters and Doctorate degrees. He is making a difference in young people's lives and is being nationally recognized for his work with underserved students. I couldn't be more proud of the young man he has become. I was crushing his spirit and I knew it.

It was time to pull out the big guns and talk it over with God. I was then at peace to guide and instruct and take on the role of support team. I wasn't attacking his spirit, I was guiding his behavior. I was at peace and that allowed him to be at peace as well.

I was specific with God. "Please help my son...." I am constantly talking things over with God from the simple "I am running late please have an open parking spot," to the heavy "God, please be with my husband during his surgery." I don't always get what I want but I always get His peace. And I have learned that that is a greater blessing. Bellow ... it's okay ... God will listen.

When it comes to your children there is a tendency to bellow too much. I like to think of parenting as "tweaking." Most of the time a "tweak" is all that is needed. If your child doesn't do their homework, a consequence based solution is in order. But if the issue is something severe such as a drug involvement, a bellow is called for. You attack the problem with guns loaded! Too often I see parents attacking their child with a full arsenal because they aren't doing their homework, yet they turn a blind eye to suspicions of drug involvement or poor friend choices. This is when you need all hands on deck and you need to fight this with everything you've got. I know a lot of wonderful parents whose kids have slipped into the drug culture and they were paying attention. It doesn't always make sense but you can't be with your child 24/7. There will be other influences in their lives that may lead them down a dark path and all the calling in world can't draw them back. It's every parents worst nightmare and I don't have any magical solutions to explain why some kids go off that path and others don't. But that is the time that you need to meet regularly with the one who is with your child every second of every day. Talk to God. Ask for His wisdom and guidance.

CHAPTER 11
Who Is Steering The Boat?

~◦~

Parenting can be the toughest, most exhausting job there is. As a parent, you are responsible for the care and management of the little ones that you bring into the world ... their wellbeing: mentally, spiritually, and physically. Each day, you not only have to be a mom or a dad but also a teacher, a nurse, a cook, a guidance counselor, a maid, a mentor, a spiritual leader, and a coach. You don't get to take days off; there are no sick days for which you can call in. Parenting is a 24 hours-a-day, seven-days-a-week job. If you work outside of the home and compound the two jobs you spell "burn out." There is little time for your own needs, much less for trying to see to the needs of your spouse. Being a parent is exhausting even on the good days, but on the days when your home is filled with chaos it can be a disaster.

It is vital that you refresh yourself and tend to your own needs so that you have enough energy and patience to care for those with whom you share your house with. I often think of parenting as being a watering can. Every day, you fill your watering can with the water that is needed for your family's well-being. Then you try to sprinkle the water on your loved ones to help them grow and give them exactly the right amount of water that they need for the day. The trouble is that life has a way of punching holes in your can, making it is nearly impossible to have enough water for each family member. There are things in life that just drain you from the moment you wake up until your head finds its way back to your pillow. Maybe you woke up late, or your child informed you that she needs something for the bake sale that afternoon. Perhaps your child's uniform is still in the gear bag in the car and he has a game today or maybe your child was up all night with a fever. All of these events can drain the water out of your watering can before your feet even leave the house.

The other challenge of parenting is that the job is constantly changing. The routine that may work for your third grader turns on its ear when your child enters junior high and the world is turned upside down. Your child who loved being with you in the younger grades is now embarrassed to be seen with their parents. They strive for independence as they get older and even though you still consider them a child they are fighting earnestly to be seen as an adult. Issues, such as a seventh grade girl wanting to shave her legs, can be all consuming for them, while you may brush it off as too early to do such a thing. As parents we need to be aware that their world is moving at a much faster rate than our world is.

We need to constantly refill our watering can so that we can have enough water to tend to the needs of our loved ones. Those needs change as our children grow so we should constantly reevaluate what is needed to keep our family healthy. But the question we have to ask is how do you stay ahead of the million and one things that will tip over your can and cause you to have hardly anything left for your family members much less for yourself?

When the responsibility of parenthood becomes overwhelming and you feel like your home is floundering, then it is time to do an evaluation of your home. Take a good assessment of what is working and what isn't. Who is in charge in your home? Too often I see parents turn their responsibility over to their kids and then wonder why there is chaos in their home. I often say to moms that if you don't step up to the plate and take charge then your two-year-old will and they lack the tools to run the house.

In sailing there can be only one skipper. Only one person gets to hold the tiller that controls the rudder and determines the direction of the boat. There will be input from the other crew members but only one person has their hand on the tiller. In marriage it may be a co-skipper arrangement where parents work as a team to present a united front. But there needs to be a clear direction of the path you are taking and what everyone's responsibilities are.

The Bible talks about the strength of the rudder and how it steers the ship in the direction it should go.

James 3:3-11

3 When we put bits into the mouths of horses to make them obey us, we can turn the whole animal. 4 Or take ships as an example. Although they are so large and are driven by strong winds, they are steered by a very small rudder wherever the pilot wants to go. 5 Likewise, the tongue is a small part of the body, but it makes great boasts. Consider what a great forest is set on fire by a small spark. 6 The tongue also is a fire, a world of evil among the parts of the body. It corrupts the whole body, sets the whole course of one's life on fire, and is itself set on fire by hell.

7 All kinds of animals, birds, reptiles and sea creatures are being tamed and have been tamed by mankind, 8 but no human being can tame the tongue. It is a restless evil, full of deadly poison.

9 With the tongue we praise our Lord and Father, and with it we curse human beings, who have been made in God's likeness. 10 Out of the same mouth come praise and cursing. My brothers and sisters, this should not be. 11 Can both fresh water and salt water flow from the same spring?

A rudder will steer a boat with just the slightest move of the tiller. It determines the direction the boat will sail. If a boat loses its rudder it is helpless and the boat will be cast about by the changing winds and a moving tide. In a boat it is vital to not only have a rudder that you can depend on, but also one that feels right in your hand. If the tiller is too loose you won't have a good feel of the changing conditions that your boat experiences and you'll lack the confidence to trust where it will take you.

Where is the rudder of your home taking you and your family? Do you allow disrespect to enter into your home? Do you have a good feel of the tiller and feel confident in the sail of your boat or is your family rudderless with no real sense of direction? The skipper determines the direction of the ship and the health of the vessel. Before sending a boat out to sea it is important to assess the condition of the boat... is it sea worthy? Are you doing that for your family? Are you guiding them and taking responsibility for the tone in your home? Do you assess the condition of the family members and yourself before you leave the house for the day? Are you doing a checklist to be sure that everyone has what they need (lifesaver, anchor, compass, etc.) to make it through the day and allow them to safely arrive back home? Is your home a safe harbor? Are all the members treated with honor and respect? Are the family members treating you with that same honor and respect? Is communication flowing freely in your home and are all members being heard? Lots of important questions to ask and that can certainly add stress to your life but it is important to get a handle on the condition of your home before you can correct any unhealthy behaviors that are present.

In many homes there doesn't seem to be a clear understanding of where they are going. Everyone is on their own and have lost their sense of direction. In order to know how you are doing, it is important to do an evaluation of the systems that you use in your home. A system is the way you communicate and how you achieve the goals that you have for your family.

Do your systems work? Is respect shown to all the family members? If not then your system isn't working. Do the children help around the house and are they responsible in doing their chores? Do you have them do chores? If your kids aren't responsible for some of the management around your home then your system isn't working.

They need ownership for the care of their home. The bottom line is that you need to evaluate the systems that you use in your home. Once you recognize those systems then you need to see if they are working. If your system isn't working then it is important to change the system. It doesn't mean that the system isn't good for it might work in someone else's home but maybe it doesn't work in yours.

You (and your spouse) are in charge of your home. It is vital to understand that and work with your spouse to cultivate systems that work for all of the family members. Once systems are in place that function properly the majority of the problems will go away. There will be things that still come up daily that you will need to address but the big items like the direction your family is traveling will be taken care of.

SYSTEMS

One of the first systems to look at is the rudder. The words that are used in your home. In cultivating homes of honor and respect it is vital to make sure that disrespect isn't running rampant in your home. If there is yelling and disrespect then your system isn't working.

We have a rule in our home that everyone is treated with respect. Our house should be everyone's safe haven and no one should feel uncomfortable in their own home. That means that I don't embarrass the kids in front of their friends, we don't use bad language, and we don't welcome guests into our home that makes the people who live there uncomfortable. If my oldest son has a friend that mocks his little brother then they aren't welcome guests until their behavior improves. Once my son invited a friend over and his behavior was rude to me. He was demanding and disrespectful to our home by jumping on the couch along with throwing something at my other son. Once he left I calmly explained to my son that his friend's behavior wasn't what I expected. He made those who lived in the home uncomfortable and as a result he wouldn't be invited back. About a month later my son requested that his friend come back over with the promise that he would behave. I agreed but let it be known that I would be paying attention. His friend was a model guest. He said please and thank you, and I noticed that his behavior was 100 percent better. What changed? When he left I asked my son and he said that he told him how to behave. He educated his friend about what a home of honor and respect looked like.

Another rule in our home is that we don't speak disrespectfully to each other. It is okay to disagree with each other and we can have different opinions, but the debate must be in a respectful manner. We don't curse, for that shows a lack of self-control. It isn't that we don't get mad or annoyed with each other but we try to be respectful in how we communicate our frustrations. I see homes where the parents yell and scream and they are surprised that the kids are out of control. They model a rudderless boat for they are out of control and they aren't giving their kids the tools to know how to navigate a boat with a firm rudder.

I expect my kids to obey. I am the parent and they aren't! If they want to take over that role then they will have that opportunity when they are older but right now this is the system we are in. I'm the mom and I get to make the rules. It is vital that an adult takes charge of your home. When you turn that responsibility over to your child and they lack the resources, then you will witness chaos. You also undermine the authority that you have and that will result in your child challenging the authority of their teachers and later in life their boss.

Respect is rule number one. This rule needs to be established early in their life. If your two year old is allowed to run around a restaurant without supervision then don't be surprised when they are disruptive every time you go to a restaurant. I don't think I ever had one of my children embarrass me in a restaurant because it just wasn't allowed. If they misbehaved, then either my husband or myself would escort them away from the table (and away from an audience) and instruct them on the proper behavior that was expected from them. I always felt that a child will misbehave up to the point of a parent's action. If the parent stays seated and doesn't make a move then the behavior the will continue, but if the parent makes a move to address the issue then the child knows that you mean business and they will respond accordingly. The threat of having to leave the table is usually enough to change the behavior. I am also sensitive to a child's attention span and realize that if they are over- tired or it is past their bedtime then they may act up. Then it may be necessary to have activities that will amuse them (rarely would I let them play with a hand held video game at the table). A game of dots or hangman on a paper placemat is acceptable but never would I let them check out of the conversation and become engaged in a game on the phone while we are out together. Too often I see not only kids, but parents as well, completely absorbed with their phone and totally ignoring their family members. This is a very bad habit to get in to and one that I would really challenge you to stay away from. Nothing is more disrespectful than to be present in someones company and have the other person tune you out over a computer screen. This is the ultimate disrespect and remember we are trying to grow home of honor and respect.

Managing your home and trying to keep order can be a challenge that I know too well with raising a daughter and three sons. I found that I was constantly frustrated with the daily chores and I rarely felt like I had my act together. It can be overwhelming to keep a house, raise four kids, and still maintain your calm. I realized that every day I felt frustrated by the work I had ahead of me and I felt like I was never done.

I once read a story about a dad that came home from work and found the kids still in their pajamas, breakfast dishes on the table and all the toys were scattered about the living room. The father asked where mom was and they told him she was up in their bedroom. He opened the door and noticed that she was reading a book and resting in bed. He asked her if she was feeling okay and she answered "Yes." He then asked what was going on. She replied "Do you know that every day you ask me what I did today ... well today I didn't do it!"

Don't you feel like that sometimes? You spend all day tending to the kids and the home and by the end of the day it feels like you didn't make any headway. Then the most frustrating thing is that you get to do it all again tomorrow. So how do you take back your life and still manage your home? My solution allowed me to feel productive but not a slave to my home. It freed up time so that I could spend more quality time with the kids and it just made me a happier person.

I developed a system that worked for me to manage the house and still feel like I had a life. My frustration was that no matter how hard I tried, I just never seemed to keep up with the work and I never felt like I was done.

In the past I would have a "to do" list in my head of all the things I needed to accomplish. Laundry, vacuum the house, dishes, make beds etc. and by the time I completed my list it was dinner time and then I got to start over again the next day. I knew that I wasn't a happy camper and my discontentment was passed on to my family. I realized that my system wasn't working and I needed to change my system.

I decided that my "to do" list was too long and basically it had the same thing on it everyday. I took back control of my home and made a daily list that I needed to accomplish and it changed each day. For example, Monday was laundry day. All I had to accomplish on Monday was tackle the laundry. A big job yes, but that was the only thing I had to do. I started early by putting a load in as soon as I got up, by the time my youngest was ready to get up I already had a load that finished drying so I took that laundry basket full of warm clothes and dumped them on him in bed. Then as I was waking him up I would fold the clothes. I can still remember him telling me "Oh mom, don't fold that one yet it was keeping my feet warm." It allowed me some one on one time with him every Monday, and I already was ahead of the game with two loads almost done. In the evening while watching Monday night football I would fold what laundry I didn't get to during the day. I even had some helpers.

Tuesday was shopping day. This was the day that I focused on my family's food needs. I cleaned out the refrigerator and I focused on making sure I had the supplies I needed for the week. I even simplified that process by asking each family member to give me five of their favorite meals that they liked to eat. I put that in a list (I had 20 meals accounted for) and I told them that they would get at least one of their meals each week. I included both my husband's and my favorites as well. What did that do for me? I just had to pick from each person's list and I had a menu for the week. I knew the supplies I needed for each meal so shopping was easy. I was no longer walking through the store trying to figure out what to make but had a plan and my system made shopping easy. Once I completed my shopping I was done for the day. My chore was complete. If I had time and wanted to tackle another chore I could but I didn't have to. I felt like I accomplished something and I was done.

Wednesday was the bathroom day. At least I knew that once a week the bathrooms were cleaned. Yes, I might have to spot clean them during the week but if I didn't get to it, it wasn't the end of the world because I knew that I would do a good cleaning on Wednesday.

Thursday was vacuuming the whole house. That required that everyone's stuff was picked up for the kids knew that they needed to have their toys and clothes off the floor for Thursday. They also knew that if I had to pick it up they may not get it back right away.

What I did was break the week down into manageable chores that allowed me to feel good and bring order to our home. I certainly enlisted the kids in helping and they knew at an early age what was expected of them. Dinnertime was a family affair. The chores for dinner were: set the table, clear the table, fill the dishwasher and wipe down the table and counters. Everyone had a job to do and that job would rotate each week. One week my daughter set the table, the next week she would clear the table and so on. When we have company my guests are always amazed that I didn't even have to ask my kids to clear the table. They just did it because they knew what was expected of them and they followed through. We developed a system that worked. There wasn't any nagging, most of the time, but there was a sense that they were part of this family and that something was expected of them.

By having order in the management of my home I was a much happier person and the home was a calmer place. In addition to my daily chore I would try each week to clean out a drawer or a closet. I would find one place that needed some organization and that was my goal for the week. I only needed to master one project each week so after awhile even that didn't seem as overwhelming. I made a point to look at the real estate in my home and make sure that rarely used items didn't command prime Real Estate. The roaster that I only used at Thanksgiving had a place in the attic, serving dishes were traded out for the season we were in. Christmas dishes were swapped out for the summer outdoor dishes. I could use the same Tupperware container in the attic and just rotate the items but I knew where to find things.

I felt like I was in control of the home instead of the home controlling me. I was happier and so were the kids. I could now spend time at their games, help with homework and just read a book. My husband was on board and together we stopped putting pressure on ourselves to have a "perfect" home and traded that in for the idea of having a "loving" home. I didn't love being a housewife for I didn't love doing chores and I didn't get a great deal of satisfaction out of getting a stain out of a carpet, but I did love being a mom. I loved everything about each stage and enjoyed watching them grow. I loved the challenges and I loved the tenderness of putting them to bed at night. If it was a beautiful day you could usually find me at the park with the kids. I wasn't going to stay home and clean the house if the outdoors were calling. Looking back I am so glad that that was my choice, for the time was so fleeting. Today I have a fairly clean home since all my kids are grown, but I would trade it in a second for the craziness, and, yes, the mess of when my kids were all home. I could count on one hand the number of games I missed watching my kids play in, for I was usually in the bleachers cheering them on. I knew their friends and they were frequent and welcomed guests in our home. By taking control of my home it brought order and fun into our lives.

Does this mean that my home was a mess? No, it was actually pretty clean. I just developed a system that worked for me. I didn't beat the kids up over their rooms but I expected them to have some order before they could have a friend over or go out. I never allowed food in their rooms and they eventually were responsible for their own laundry. It took time but soon the systems were in place and we were a fairly smooth-running machine.

I tried to make a point of having most of my chores done before the kids came home so that when they walked in the door I was available for them if they needed me. I usually had a snack waiting for them and I tried to give them time to regroup after a hard day before the pressures of homework was put on their shoulders. One of my sons had a teacher who would give you the homework for the week with the instruction to do one sheet a night. She understood that life was busy for these kids so if you knew that you had a game on Wednesday night you might want to do double homework on Tuesday night. I loved her for that. She taught my son time management in third grade!

That was essentially what I was doing. I was bringing time management into my home. I was still working part time at the Medical Center so I needed to know my schedule ahead of time and then plan accordingly. It brought order and structure into our home and everyone was better off because of it.

A few other tools to help you in your home management is to have a spot for each child's gear. We had a closet that we divided into quarters and each child had their own cubicle. That was where their shoes, coat, book bag and anything else they might need could be found. We tried to make sure that we organized the night before so we weren't rushed in the morning especially with a 7 a.m. bus pickup.

It is important to get the kids onboard early in their lives so they know that something is expected of them. When I ran the sailing program, each student was responsible for the rigging and unrigging of the boat they were using. Some of these kids were as young as 6 years old and they were taught how to remove the mast, roll the sail, and put the gear away. When my son was the instructor he told the kids to not ask their parents for help. They were old enough to do it themselves, but if they needed help they were to ask a teammate or the instructor. He said that most of the parents weren't sailors and they probably didn't know how to do it anyway. They were to learn for themselves and know when to ask for help. To watch these little kids carry their gear to the sailing locker was a sight to behold. The parents were amazed and often said that they couldn't even get their kids to clear their plate from the table but watching how they took responsibility for their boat was impressive. That was because something was expected of them. They were told the proper routine and they were expected to follow through. There wasn't any yelling or punishment given just an understanding that this was part of the expectations of sailing a boat.

Why don't we have the same expectations with our kids in our own homes? They need to learn to pitch in and help and eventually anticipate the needs of others. They need to understand that they can disagree but they must be respectful in the process. If they want to plead a case, then expect them to do it in an age appropriate manner. If your son is 16 and acting like a two-year-old then he should be treated like a two-year-old. If he asks like a 16- year-old then respond like you would to an adult. In my home, I will have one response for a toddler and another response for a teenager, so they need to learn to behave accordingly.

When a teenager asks for something like going to a party, instead of a "yes" or a "no" response I might ask them to "convince me" to let them go. Let them use their words and explain themselves. If they tell me it's because everyone is going, then I might respond that that isn't even close to a valid argument, keep trying. I want them to develop critical thinking so they can make wise choices. As a matter of fact we used that word a lot: "wise."

I want them to understand what it means to make wise decisions and to constantly seek wisdom. The problem is that often parents don't demonstrate wise choices themselves and as a result the kids follow in their footsteps. The scriptures tell us to be seekers of wisdom.

Proverbs 14:1
The wise woman builds her house, but with her own hands the foolish one tears hers down.

Proverbs 16:16
How much better to get wisdom than gold, to choose understanding rather than silver!

Proverbs 19:11
Sensible people control their temper; they earn respect by overlooking wrongs.

Proverbs 19:11
Sensible people control their temper; they earn respect by overlooking wrongs.

Proverbs 19:20
Listen to advice and accept instruction, and in the end you will be wise.

Proverbs 29:11
A fool gives full vent to his anger, but a wise man keeps himself under control.

Proverbs 29:15
To discipline a child produces wisdom, but a mother is disgraced by an undisciplined child.

James 1:5
If any of you lacks wisdom, he should ask God, who gives generously to all without finding fault, and it will be given to him.

When you take control of the rudder in your home you will see amazing things happen. The path you are steering will be clear and purposeful. The members of your home will understand their job and what is expected of them and therefore the journey will be smoother. You will develop more confidence as you feel the tiller in your hand and know that you are directing the outcome of your family.

CHAPTER 12

Rocky Shores And Strong Currents

Sailing can be such an enjoyable sport or pastime as you enjoy the fresh breeze and open waters. Sometimes you just feel the wind on your face and love the ease which makes your boat sail through the water. When you master the art of sailing you don't even have to pay much attention to the details that once consumed you when you first learned the sport. You know when to trim the sails or bear off with the breeze. It is almost like being on auto pilot and you can keep your eyes out of the boat. You can just enjoy the joy of being on the water.

But it is vital to be able to be able to look around and anticipate potential trouble. "To keep your eyes outside the boat." It is important to pay attention to the conditions around you so that you can ward off danger or sail smoothly around trouble. If a fisherman is anchored you will need to alter your course before you are right on top of them. If the shoreline is rocky you will need to be aware of the hidden dangers located below the surface. Watching for wind allows you to anticipate if a strong gust is headed your way. If you are sailing in the middle of the lake, you do need to be on the lookout for other vessels and unexpected wind shifts that are impacted by the shoreline. Usually, it is just a side note and something you are aware of but not panicked about. As a matter of fact, many times you sail without much thought about it, as it is something that you just respond to that allows you to avoid a collision.

That changes if the tack you are on takes you close to the shoreline or you are sailing in waters that have a strong currents. Then you need you to be more attentive to your surroundings. We sail in a glacial lake that has a very rocky base to it. In some areas the water is quite deep but in other places there are steep cliffs that angle down into the water. If you sail up to the shoreline and your rudder hits, it can spell disaster as there is the potential for the rocky ledge to sheer off your rudder and leave you floundering with no way to navigate the boat. When we have visitors to the lake, our race committee informs the competitors where the dangerous shoreline is to make sure that they don't suffer that scary fate.

When raising children, most of the time it is smooth sailing. Oh sure, there are many, many bumps along the way, but for the most part it is a simple power struggle with you exercising your rights as the parent over your child's rights in a battle of wills. But there will be times, especially during the teenage years, where you find yourself right up against the rocky shores. If you don't navigate well you can find yourself in major damage without a clear direction on how to proceed.

It is vital that you become aware of the shoreline before you send your child off on their own. To be informed about where the dangers are and to help your child be aware of the dangers as well. It is important to know where the rocks are that can sink your child's boat and leave them powerless to help themselves. Some rocks are above the water and very obvious, like the dangers of drugs, but others are hidden just below the surface like a toxic friendship that can destroy a child's self esteem or lead them astray. It is important to pay attention and to be on constant watch for these dangers and to help your child be aware of them ahead of time.

When we were raising our children, more often than not, our home was the place that always seemed to have a large gang of kids in it. With four kids plus their friends over, there were times that it seemed a bit crazy, but we loved it. At least I did, I know sometimes my husband wasn't so sure. I wanted to have an open-door policy that was welcoming so that I would know who my kids' friends were and what they were up to, even though it was exhausting. I always had a cupboard full of food that I could make in a moments notice such as pasta or frozen pizzas.

I actually loved picking my kids up after a day of practice or a game. It allowed me a glimpse into their world. I was usually driving one or more extra kids home and as they sat in the back seat talking I could quietly drive and just listen to what they were saying. I tried to avoid asking too many questions because I wanted them to forget that I was there so that they could talk freely. You can gain a lot of information about your kids by just listening. Something that I noted was that when they first came out of the school door, they were full of jabber, but by the time they got home they were ready to go to their room and decompress. The window into their world was closed a bit and I didn't have the same access as I did on the drive.

I found myself always looking for opportunities to hear what was going on in their world. By going to their games, I was able to interact with other parents. I could get a sense if things were going okay or if there was something I needed to be aware of. It also allowed me the opportunity to talk about a play or the other team's reaction to something with my child at dinner. I could ask about their teammates and what did they think about so-and-so's goal or how they got hurt. I was let into their world for a small bit of their life and I was going to cherish it.

Another thing that I have found invaluable was having dinner together. Sitting around the table is a wonderful time when you get to regroup as a family and touch base with one another. It was a time where we put away the hassles of the day and just enjoyed some time together. There were a few rules at our table, and number one was that we didn't start eating until everyone was seated. I served a family-style dinner and you didn't begin to serve up your plate until everyone was there and we had a chance to thank the Lord. This was our opportunity to pause and reconnect with each other and with God. It gave us the chance to talk about our day and assess the health and well being of each family member. If one of my children was out of sorts at the table then I knew I needed to pay special attention to them later that evening. It was a chance to watch them interact with each other and tell their stories.

I remember once as we were having dinner and everyone was talking (we did have a very chatty family), my youngest child found that he was having trouble breaking into the conversation. Finally, he put his hands in the air and said "When I do this everyone stop talking!" We all just looked at him and got a kick out of the fact that he was finally getting a voice. I think he was startled that we all stopped talking and he felt the need to say something. With us all staring at him he said, "Apples have vitamins, lots of vitamins, especially in the skin!" Then abruptly his hands went down and he went back to his plate. Well you can imagine our reaction, but it was something that we all remembered and it marked the day that the baby developed a voice at the table.

The family meal is so important and something that requires effort. Yes, it is easier to just throw something in front of them and let them watch TV, but the effort to have a family meal is worth it tenfold. When I mentioned this at one of our Lighthouse sessions, a mom of two boys said that they just couldn't seem to find the time to have dinner together but she would try. She came back a week later and said that it was amazing. The first two nights were hard and she kept saying to herself, after she put in a long day as a teacher, "Is this worth it?" But after the third night, her boys opened up and she heard about their days. They got used to the routine and now felt safe to share. She told me that if they didn't have dinner together she wouldn't have know about some of the things that were going on in their world. She said that in such a short time she saw the value and so did her husband. It's not easy, but believe me you will be glad that you made the effort.

Some of the requirements that I had at the table, as I mentioned before, were that everyone had a job in the meal preparation. Way too often I see children treat their parents like nothing more than their maids. By expecting something of them they learned that they are part of the family and with that they had responsibilities. If they didn't set the table, the food came out anyway and we all sat around the table watching our food get cold until the person who was supposed to set the table got the plates. They needed to see that without them doing their job everyone suffers. Life lessons.

If you can't do a family dinner then try for breakfast together, even if it is only on the weekends. Look for opportunities to all be present around the table and regroup. I can still remember Sunday dinners growing up. We went to church and then came home to a lazy Sunday, reading the funnies in the newspaper and watching a football game on TV. The roast was cooking and we had dinner around 2 p.m. Later it was a supper of soup and sandwiches. It was comforting to be together and just be lazy. So often the world is too busy to pause like that, so you need to find every opportunity you can to regroup as a family.

A tradition that we had in our home was serving dinner on a "red plate." It was one lone red plate that was used if a family member was being honored. If it was your birthday, if you won an award, or you passed a hard test, then you were entitled to eat your meal on the "red plate." When the kids came to the table and saw that the red plate was at their seat you could tell that they were excited. They were being honored.

It is important to carve memories and special moments into your everyday routine. Life goes by so quickly so it is important to allow pauses in your crazy routine and bring calmness to your children's lives. It also creates traditions that they may pass down to the next generation.

God told us in the Commandments to take a day of rest. "Remember the Sabbath and keep it Holy." He knew that we needed a day to pause and regroup. Even Jesus needed to disconnect from His world and go off by Himself to pray and regroup. God challenges us to slow down and focus on the truly important things in life. I often think of life as a long, run- on sentence that seems to go on and on without a proper period. When you were younger you were taught the importance of proper punctuation in your writing.

You shouldn't let a sentence just ramble on and on without breaking it up into two sentences or using punctuations, such as a comma, to make sense of what you were writing about.

I challenge you to take a look at your life and assess the condition of your journey. Is your life a continuous run on sentence with no pauses to slow your world down? If it is, then you need to look for opportunities to add commas and maybe a good old semicolon to your life. I think of commas as outings with friends, family dinners, a call to your parents, etc. Things that allow you to slow down and enjoy the journey. A semicolon are those once in a lifetime moments that you pause to celebrate — a birthday, an anniversary, a family trip etc. —moments that will forge memories for a lifetime. Look for opportunities to find the punctuation that your family needs to keep it healthy and balanced.

During the writing of this book the world experienced the Covid-19 virus shutdown and the forced pausing of our world. As unsettling and in some cases tragic as it is, the blessing that I see is a reconnection with the ones you love. A forced slowdown and a reevaluation of what is truly important. The things that we thought were so important were pushed aside and families enjoyed dinner together. Life events were altered and weddings became small intimate gatherings, love was shown by a car parade, and Zoom conferences became a way to connect with loved ones.

There are so many things that can pull your family apart and that it why it is important to look for any and all opportunities to keep them together. When my boys played lacrosse, all age levels played on the same day against the same town. My solution to having to spend a whole day on the lacrosse field was to pack a picnic lunch. We all were together so why not have a family picnic? Many times we had extra guests but we paused together and regrouped as a family.

Prayer at the table was also important. We never began our meal without a word of thanks to the Lord. The prayer could be a simple memorized prayer or just some words from the heart. We took turns saying grace and no one put a drop of food on their plate until we thanked the Lord. I did notice some jockeying of the food so that they had the mashed potatoes closest to them and when the prayer was done they got to get the first scoop. Prayer allowed us to pause and refocus our attention on his provisions.

Some of our favorite prayers were:

Thank you for the world so sweet,
Thank you for the food we eat,
Thank you for the birds that sing,
Thank you God for everything.

Or

Bless us oh Lord,
and these thy gifts
which we are about to receive,
From thy bounty
through Christ our Lord, Amen

If it was a prayer from the heart it may be something like this:

Dear Lord,
Thank you for the blessings that you provide for our family
We ask that you bless grandma with your healing hands and help her through her upcoming surgery.
Please help us feel your presence tomorrow during our very busy day.
We ask this in your name
Amen

It is important to be alert to what is going on in your home. Whenever we had a gang of kids at our house, I found that it was important to be on watch for activities that could lead to trouble. But how do you do that without looking like a nag? It required being present yet unseen. I might teach them a card game and play with them, or take them on an adventure to the local park. A trick that I used when they got bigger and they didn't want me hanging around was to always have a giant tub of chocolate chip cookie dough in the refrigerator. If I had a group of kids playing in the basement I would make one batch and then bring down a plate of warm chocolate chip cookies right out of the oven. I would offer each child a cookie and while I did that I would look in their eyes to be sure they looked clear, I would be smelling their breath to be sure I didn't detect that they had been smoking, and if it was a co-ed gathering, I was looking at their lips to be sure they didn't look puffy which meant that they were kissing. Oh course, they didn't know that I was doing all that, they just thought that I was offering them a warm cookie. I also only made one batch at a time. So when I went back upstairs, I put in another batch and 20 minutes later, I offered them another warm cookie. My kids may not have always been happy to see my feet coming down the stairs but none of their friends minded that I was there with another plate of warm cookies.

I wanted my home to be a safe place and I would welcome my kids friends in frequently. Some days it would get a bit old but I knew the value of letting them hang out in a safe environment. It was funny, one day I went downstairs and my kid's friends were hanging out eating sub sandwiches that they picked up at the local deli. That was fine, but none of my own kids were home. I teased them and asked what they were all doing there. They responded that their parents didn't get mad if they knew that they were at our house. I was a responsible, but fun, adult. The ultimate compliment!

They felt welcomed and they knew that we cared about them. I drove them, supported them and listened to them. As they got older I even got phone calls at 2 a.m. asking for a ride home from the bar. They said to me as they got in my car, "Thanks Mrs. K, next time you need a DD we'll be there for you!" I loved it and thankfully never needed it. The point was that they knew that I would be there for them. As I look back on that chapter I can remember how exhausting it was worrying about all four of my kids and then their friends on top of it but that was part of the job I signed up for when I became a parent.

Yes, it required a lot of effort and lots and lots of patience, but as I look back it was worth every second. I saw a Facebook post by one of my Lighthouse ladies whose son was getting ready to go off to college. It showed a picture of her mud room and a mountain of shoes. She said "As I arrived home today, I saw a pile of shoes by my door that were not just the shoes of my boys. I knew that my refrigerator would be empty, and my couch would be full of 180 pound men with empty soda cans all around them. There would be wet towels by the pool and the back door would probably be left wide open, but I didn't care. By the end of the week these men would be traveling all across the country going to different schools and universities. Their life would never be the same and the memories of their High School years would be cemented by moments like this. I will long for those shoes by the door and the cans all over my living room. So for today, I will just sit back and watch the mess and take joy in the fact that they are home in my house."

Why are all of these moments important? Because it helps you to know where the rocks are and which way the current is flowing. You need to be engaged in your child's life to see the hazards that may lie ahead. There are so many obstacles that can damage your child's boat, so it is vital that you are constantly assessing the vessel and the watching the changing shorelines. If you are aware of the dangers then you are able to prepare yourself and your child for the damage that may lie ahead.

The interesting thing about raising children is that they are constantly changing. Every year in your child's life they become a different person. The changes from year to year can be like the currents that flow and are ever moving. This change in your child typically occurs in the fall when they reenter the school after a lazy summer. When they take their place in a higher grade where more is expected of them. Their classroom full of students will change and the routine that they were familiar with is different. This is when you will see the change register most sharply and their world is a bit off kilter. The funny thing is that most parents don't think about this at all. They think that their sweet sixth grader will begin seventh grade just as agreeable and just as talkative. They are then shocked when their child starts to sass them and they begin to spend more and more time alone in their room. They fail to see that everyone has changed and moved a rung up the ladder.

When I teach grand-parenting class, I need to remind the new grandparents of this change. Parents are now grandparents, and kids are now parents. Everyones role has changed and their attitudes and responsibilities have changed with that move. Our goal is to be aware of the changes and to assess how everyone is navigating the different environment.

That is what happens each year of your child's life. They are on a constant moving journey and too often, we as parents fail to adjust to the move. Frequently, I see parents doing too much for their children and not adjusting to the child's need to grow and learn. They constantly treat a 12-year-old as a child and forget that they are beginning the adjustment into adulthood. It is important to keep refocusing on each of your children and try to understand what their needs are at each new stage.

The flow of the currents constantly move and change directions. What worked for your child at age seven may not work for them at age twelve. That is why it is vital to have some traditions and constants that can anchor your child and help them navigate the changing waters. Dinner together, attending church, praying, family traditions, using the red plate, all help a child feel connected to the family. You may get some push back on some issues but don't lose hope, continue down the path and realize that some of those traditions will be vital when they leave home and need something to anchor to.

I just watched a foreign commercial about a new father dancing to a song with his newborn son. The next scene was him dancing to the same song with his toddler and the little boy was laughing and dancing along with the music. Next the boy was older and just smiled at the father's dancing. This was followed by a scene in a coffee shop where the music was playing and the father got up and danced to the old familiar song and you could see that the son was mortified. The last scene was the parents sitting alone around their Christmas tree and one of the packages started ringing. The father opened it up and there was his son and new grandson on the phone screen with the old familiar song playing. Miles away three generations danced to the music with pure and simple joy.

The currents that are the most dangerous are the turbulent flows when two bodies of water meet. The East River in New York City is notorious for dangerous eddies and monstrous undertows. It is the fight between the two flowing rivers that create havoc and require the boat handler to pay extra attention to the drama. That is the adolescence experience. There are two opposing forces that are at battle with each other. Childhood verses adulthood are at play and the pull from each direction is tremendously strong. They are caught in the middle and if left unprepared for the changes they could be pulled under. They need to enter this chapter in their life with some wisdom and understanding about what is happening to their world.

I had a tradition in my family, and I have shared it with many others, of the importance of having "The Talk" when my child hits the age of 10 … the double digits. It may seem very young to have "the talk" but believe me in their world they are already entering turbulent waters. If not them then maybe their friends are changing and your child may not be sure how to handle it.

I begin by letting them know that something special is going to happen on their 10th birthday. When that day arrives we begin by going out for a special lunch, just the two of us. We then go to the drugstore and buy a shopping cart full of the supplies that they will need as their body goes through the changes that come with puberty. Some of the items include deodorant, nail clippers, face wash, a razor and sanitary supplies for the girls. We buy a container to store their items in and I tell them that they may not need these things today but in the near future they will need them so I want them prepared. They will know that they need deodorant when they realize that after gym class they smell. They will need face wash when they start to see signs of acne etc. When they start to use these items remind them to let you know so that you can restock their kit.

The last step of the day is to inform them of the changes that will be taking place with their bodies. I talk about the gift of sex and that it is the closest that two people can ever be with each other and that it is a special gift from God and not something to do with someone as a party game. It is a delicate talk but informative and I encourage you to use the proper language. I tell them that I want them to know what is happening to their bodies and that they aren't to share this talk with their classmates. Hopefully, your friend's parents will be talking to them just as I am talking to you. But most importantly, I want you to hear about it from us, your parents. I want my children to have the correct information and I want it to be framed as a sign that they are maturing. This is also a good time to talk about a new level of communication. In the past I treated you as a child, but today I want to start treating you as a young adult and as a result we need to learn how to communicate. "If you want to be treated as a teenager then you must communicate as one." If they need space they need to ask for it. If they want to go someplace, they need to convince me and if they are angry with me they need to tell me what is wrong. Slamming doors is not communication.

I did this with each of my children and I feel like it helped them understand what was happening to their bodies and to their friends. I find if you wait until they are twelve or older they are embarrassed by the conversation and in most cases they have already experienced many changes or have seen those changes in their friends.

Helping them to understand the pulls in their lives will help them to be empowered to navigate the turbulent waters and be attentive to the changes. Most of the time, the adjustments of parenting are minor tweaks but if you see something more dangerous occurring like drugs, violence or sexual immorality then you need to attack it with your guns loaded and perhaps some extra help. Don't turn a blind eye if you suspect your child is going under. You need to act quickly and with purpose. You need to be in touch with other parents and see if they have any insight into what is going on. By the way, NEVER, and I mean NEVER, reveal the sources of your information. Your child must never know how and where you get your information from. If you tell them that Joey's mom told you, then you have put up a guard against Joey's mom and also caused friction between Joey and his mom.

It is important to have many sources and to verify before you act. My job as a mom is to be a wisdom seeker. That means if I hear something I search for the truth. I investigate and get as much information as possible before I react. I am a gatherer of details and try to get the whole picture before I make a judgement. This also helps me make wiser decisions.

If my child asks a question and I am not sure of the answer then I simply say that I will get back to them. As a parent sometimes you feel like you need to give an answer immediately but I want you to realize that taking a step away from the situation and gaining wisdom will help you handle things better. You will gain perspective and it will help you to not overreact. "Let me think this over," "Let me talk to your father about the situation," "Let me see what your teacher has to say about what happened." All valid and all buy you time.

Church was important to our family and we valued that time as a family unit. Traditions and a community beyond ourselves help to strengthen the family and the activities that the church had for the youth built a strong sense of community, support, and giving. If you lack a family church, I encourage you to find a religious community that cultivates your family's faith and allows you the opportunity to experience traditions and fellowship with others. It's easy to just let the Sunday morning go without having to get dressed and attending worship but what you are missing is priceless. To be with a community of faith believers and people that care about your well being in invaluable. To have your children in a program that tills the soil of their faith is the most important gift that I can imagine giving to your child. I hear parents say that they want their children to be able to "choose" what religion they want to be. That is the biggest copout that I have ever heard. Sure, the choice to be part of God's family will ultimately be their decision but while I am growing them, I will do everything in my power to till their soil.

How can they make a decision, if you don't give them the tools to choose one choice over another.

There is something called Pascal's wager. Blaise Pascal was a 17th century philosopher, mathematician and physicist who developed an argument in philosophy. He states that humans bet with their lives that God either exists or does not. His rational was very simple, you have a choice and then there are the consequences. He reasons that you must place a wager, that is not optional. You must make a choice.

The four options are:

* ***You believe in God, and He exists.*** What are the consequences? Everlasting life, peace on the journey, comfort and sense of belonging.

* ***You believe in God and He doesn't exists.*** You end up in the ground. You experienced peace, and comfort while on the journey but in the end you were just reduced to dirt. At least you had comfort on the journey.

* ***You do not believe in God and He doesn't exists.*** You didn't feel His presence while on earth and in the end you just became dirt in the ground.

* ***You do not believe in God and He does exist.*** You lost out on feeling His presence and peace during your time on the earth and you lose out on His promise of everlasting life. A pretty big consequence especially when you are talking about eternity.

Let us weigh the gain and loss in wagering that God exists. If you gain, you gain all; if you lose, you lose nothing. That means that one can gain eternal life if God exists, but if not, one will be no worse off in death than if one had not believed. On the other hand, if you bet against God, win or lose, you either gain nothing or lose everything. You either experience death as an ending with a burial in the ground or miss the opportunity of eternal happiness.

It appears that one point is settled. Wager, then, without hesitation that He exists.

Hebrews 11:1 *Now faith is confidence in what we hope for and assurance about what we do not see.*

The journey that your child is on will have lots of twists and turns and unfortunately you can't protect them from every danger on their travels, but you can prepare them for some of the dangers and changes that they may encounter. That is why it is important for you to keep your eyes open and be alert for teachable moments when you can share some wisdom with your child.

CHAPTER 13

The Journey Home

Your child is starting to feel confident in their skills and beginning to leave the nest and sailed away from the safe harbors. They have taken that step in life where you are no longer there at every turn, at least physically, to help them manage their boat. They spend more time away from you and there are others that will step in and serve as role models or influences in their life.

As we prepare our child for their journey, it is important to let them know that they can find rest in the comfort of your home. After a long day on the water sometimes nothing feels as wonderful as seeing the harbor in the distance and knowing that the comfort of shore is waiting for you. It is there that you can pause from the constant struggles of manning your boat and the constant need to watch the weather. As relaxing as sailing can be, you need to be constantly aware of your surroundings and the changing conditions that you are exposed to. You can't let your guard down or you may find that you are a moment away from disaster. If you are sailing toward a beautiful blue sky with the harbor behind you, you may not realize that storm clouds are building over your back and developing between you and the safety you crave. A constant checking of the conditions around you is always necessary so that you aren't taken by surprise.

There are challenges out in this world that you can't prepare for, things that can blind-side you and take you by surprise like a medical diagnosis, or a death in the family. These are situations where no amount of preparation will equip you to handle things by yourself. It brings with it the sudden need to call out for help as you realize that your strength isn't enough to carry the burden. Having a support team that will lift you up in prayer and love when you are feeling completely spent will help you during your time of need.

I met a woman this morning at church who is going through cancer treatments. She said it was the toughest thing that she has ever gone through but her family, friends, and church have embraced her and let her know how loved she was. She said that she has two more treatments before her upcoming surgery and that she knew that she needed to be at church and feel God's presence and thank Him for allowing her to know the gift of support that she was given. Wow, she is in the middle of her treatment and she is able to see the blessings in her life ... that is God's joy! It doesn't mean that she wasn't blindsided by the storm but she had the right team in her boat. They helped her sail to the harbor and now she can rest.

I challenge you to take a good look at your home. What is the tone in your house? Is it one of comfort and support or one of anger and strife? I am not asking if you have a home with a perfect spouse and wonderful well behaved children. I am not asking if you came from a perfect childhood yourself or if you had scars from your time as a child. What I am asking is what is the tone of YOUR home? Is the overall tone one of love and support? Do the members feel safe coming in the door? Is the light burning for each member to come home after a long day on the water? Does everyone feel comfortable in their boat and do they have what it takes to manage it on their own? Do they remember to take their anchor, life jacket, and compass with them each day or are they hoping for the best? Is the overall tone upbeat and happy or accusing and angry? Be honest with yourself about the condition of your home so that you can begin today to change it if it is needed.

I like to think of mothers as the barometer in the homes. A barometer lets you know what the atmospheric pressure is and lets you know if a storm is coming. When a mom is in a good place and allows her relational strengths to thrive, she behaves like a good and loyal barometer. She can pick up on the subtle changes in the home and forecast that something is brewing. She can tell that her daughter is off the minute she comes in the door from school. There is something that goes off in her that signals a storm is brewing and preparation and care is needed. Likewise, when her son leaves the field of play, just his greeting can let her know what his esteem level is. She can tell that he liked how he preformed or that he felt like he let himself and the team down. If a mom is in a good place she can be invaluable to the wellbeing of the home for she is attune to the subtle changes and able to head off situations before they become major storms.

A father on the other hand is a valuable asset in helping to solve the problems that arise in the family. They are natural problem solvers and once aware that a situations exists they are great at looking at the issue objectively and finding a solution. Many times they don't get overwhelmed by the small details and tend to look at things from a "big picture" viewpoint.

Together this team works well at managing a home. When parents are both in a good place it can be like watching a well choreographed dance. Sometimes one leads and the other follows and sometimes the roles are reversed. They can work together, using each others' strengths, and do what is necessary for the well-being of the entire home.

Problems arise when spouses don't value the unique makeup of each other or when one spouse doesn't step up or is too overwhelmed to even know what their role is or sadly is absent altogether. I see this way too often and I know how overwhelming it is for a family when everyone is in their own place of chaos and no one finds rest in the home. Each person is traveling aimlessly with no sense of purpose and no safe haven to rest in. This is what God tells us is a lack of peace. Anxiety is another word that can describe this situation. As I look around I see a world full of anxious people. Everyone is in a storm and no one knows where to go for safety and rest. I hear all the time, "I'm just so tired." Even in their own home they can't find peace. They don't feel rest at bedtime and so they begin another day tired, anxious and without a destination.

If this describes your family I want you to know that there is hope. I love that word! HOPE!

H… Home … the promise that there is someplace for you to rest and feel love.

O … Opportunity … God has plans for you and today the opportunity is there to change the tone in your home and make it a safe haven for you and your loved ones.

P … Peace … The world is so loud. Come to God and feel His peace and enjoy the idea of "resting in His presence." He wants to calm you and talk to you. He wants you to pause and listen to what He has to say and where He wants you to go.

E … Environment … He wants you to experience the transforming power that finding a safe harbor can give you. He wants you to know the way home and He wants you to rest here each and every night. He wants to fill your head with His word and write on your heart His promises. He wants you to feel confident to leave the shore every day but knowing where to return when the sun sets.

HOPE … A transforming power that begins with you calling out for help. God wants to work with you and He already knows that you have what it takes because He entrusted you with His priceless possessions, His children. He asked you to care for them and guide them, but one day He will call each and everyone of His children home. Make sure that you and your family knows the way home.

So, how do you achieve this peace and hope that God promises? It is actually quite simple, you ask Him for it. When you finally say, "God, I can't do this alone", then He is there to guide and support you.

When I was running the junior sailing program, there was a boy who was afraid during his lesson as the wind picked up a bit and he was alone in his boat. He was starting to get anxious and he kept shouting that he couldn't do it and he wanted to get into the instructor's boat. My son, being the sailing instructor, came up beside him and told him that he could do it. "You have the tools you need to sail this boat but I will stay beside you for the journey home." That boy successfully sailed home and gained a new confidence that would carry him through the rest of the summer. God is asking the same thing of you. You have the tools that you need but you may be forgetting to call out God's name to sail beside you. To be with you every step of the journey.

The next thing I challenge you to look at is what are the goals for your family? Where are you going? You can't reach your goals if you don't know what they are. In sailing you have to know the direction of the wind before you can adjust your sails. If the wind is behind you you can sail straight for your mark but if you encounter a headwind, then you have to tack back and forth to reach your goal. That is a what life is like. Sometimes your life is a smooth and easy sail but other times obstacles and detours send you off away from where you have to go. There is a need for constant readjusting to climb the wind to make some forward progress.

As a parent it is important to have goals for your family. Mantras that your family lives by such as "Cultivating homes of honor and respect," or "In this house we first serve the Lord" ...sayings that let everyone know where your family is headed. By having a family mantra everyone knows where the safety of the harbor is and how to get there.

Goals ... If you aim at nothing you will hit is every time. When you hear of the wonderful success stories by many of the top achievers in our world, often it was the love they felt during the trials that made them succeed. Thomas Edison was told that he wouldn't amount to much by his teachers in grammar school so his mom, who saw his potential, home- schooled him. Experiencing her love he went on to become a world famous inventor who looked at everything as a possibility, just like his mom. Ben Carson, a noted neurosurgeon, began his life in the projects but had a mom who knew that through education he could leave his surroundings and achieve great things. She challenged him to greatness.

Money, fame, and power aren't what God looks for. He is interested in your heart. We live in a world that is filled with false advertising. If you buy this, you'll be happy. If only I lived in that home, I'd be happy. If only my spouse was more attentive, I'd be happy. God challenges us to look at the world through His eyes. He wants your heart right and then you will experience peace, joy, love, patience, self-control, goodness, kindness, gentleness and faith. The Fruits of the Spirit. Gal 5:22.

I think those are some pretty good goals to strive for. God tells us that we don't have to go searching for these things alone. He'll be beside you to help you find them. By asking for patience when our kids are driving us crazy, or asking for love when our spouse is annoying us, He gives us the first step to achieving a wisdom and peace that we would never even thought possible.

The Bible tells us that we are to be His children and He wants to be our Father. What exactly does that mean? When you think about what the world was like when Jesus was walking on the earth, children were not valued. Children and women were reduced to second-class citizens, yet throughout the Gospels both women and children were valued by Jesus. Women were the first to see the empty tomb, children were called to sit at Jesus's feet. A boy with a lunch pail fed the multitudes when Jesus turned his lunch of a loaf of bread and some fish into enough food to feed the crowd with baskets left over. Jesus saw the value of the helpless and empowered them to do great things. He can do the same for you.

Today ask God to be your Father. What do you get in return? A father who loves and cares for you and wants the best for you and your family. When you think about little children you realize that they aren't in charge of anything. Their parents determine when and what they can eat, what they wear, and when they go to bed. They really don't have much of a say in many aspects of their life, yet most children are delightfully happy. On the other hand, adults who are in charge of so much have a tendency to be miserable. Look at people in a supermarket, they have an unbelievable assortment of food to choose from and yet they are so unhappy. They have money but are always fretting and searching for more. What is the difference? Adults think they are in charge and feel like they need to keep the world running. Children know they aren't and allow their parents to provide for them. God is asking you to rest in that same knowledge. He's got it, so you can rest and let Him keep the world running.

Children also are famous for always asking for things. They aren't afraid to ask for a pony for Christmas or a candy bar at the store. They aren't afraid to lift their arms up to ask for a hug or crawl into a parents lap when they are tired. They are always asking for stuff, it's just what they do. Sometimes parents will answer their requests with a "yes" and sometimes it is "no" or "not now", but it doesn't stop the child from asking. God tells us the same thing. Ask and you shall receive, seek and you shall find, knock and the door will be opened.

God longs for you to seek Him, to ask Him for stuff and to knock at His door. There is a beautiful painting that shows Jesus knocking at a door just outside a garden. The interesting thing about the painting is that there isn't a door handle on Jesus' side of the door. What does it mean? That we are the ones who have to open the door. He is there waiting but we have to take the step of opening the door to let him in. If your world is falling apart or just a bit unraveling, pause and ask God to enter into your home. You don't have to clean it up or be perfect to invite Him in. Consider it a "Come as You Are" party where everyone arrives today just as they are. The transformation in your home will occur by His presence and you'll be amazed by the peace you will feel over time. When meeting a new friend, the conversation at first may be forced and awkward but soon the conversation begins to flows and the relationship becomes easy. I want to tell you that there is no greater friend, listener, problem solver, and lover than God. Ask Him in, you won't be sorry.

Another thing that babies do is they like to nap. They need refreshing and they get cranky if they don't get enough sleep. Nothing is better than when we feel well rested and we get a chance to "sleep like a baby." But unfortunately, too many adults are robbed of this gift and fret all night. They are anxious and don't know how to rest. Anxiety causes distraction and a choking or strangling feeling. It is a painful uneasiness due to an impending fear. It is a mental, emotional, and spiritual strangulation and at its mildest, we churn and at its worst we panic. The beginning of anxiety is the end of faith. Anxiety highlights our own need to be in control and strangles the divine. We become fearful when we know that we can't do things on our own and that leads to panic. It also chokes our ability to think straight. We can't determine what is incidental and what is essential. We overreact, and we don't see clearly. We make mountains out of molehills and then don't see the real traps before us or our family. We lose our way. We also fail to grow fruit since worry strangles our heart and we can't relax. We don't allow the Holy Spirit into our lives and as a result we find ourselves empty. Worry robs us of our energy and joy and that results in making us judgmental rather than accepting, so we become negative. Our anxiety stems from a desire to be in control, being afraid to let go of the past, or forgive those that harmed us. We fail to trust God and therefore our faith is lacking. When we learn that we can depend on the Lord to handle the people and circumstances of our lives, then the outcome will be an existence free of worry, anxiety and fear. It is then that peace will flow like a river through us.

Matthew 6:25-34
Do Not Worry
25 *"Therefore I tell you, do not worry about your life, what you will eat or drink; or about your body, what you will wear.*

Is not life more than food, and the body more than clothes? **26** *Look at the birds of the air; they do not sow or reap or store away in barns, and yet your heavenly Father feeds them. Are you not much more valuable than they?* **27** *Can any one of you by worrying add a single hour to your life?*
28 *"And why do you worry about clothes? See how the flowers of the field grow. They do not labor or spin.* **29** *Yet I tell you that not even Solomon in all his splendor was dressed like one of these.* **30** *If that is how God clothes the grass of the field, which is here today and tomorrow is thrown into the fire, will he not much more clothe you—you of little faith?* **31** *So do not worry, saying, 'What shall we eat?' or 'What shall we drink?' or 'What shall we wear?'* **32** *For the pagans run after all these things, and your heavenly Father knows that you need them.* **33** *But seek first his kingdom and his righteousness, and all these things will be given to you as well.* **34** *Therefore do not worry about tomorrow, for tomorrow will worry about itself. Each day has enough trouble of its own.*

God wants to spend some time with you. He wants to refresh you and allow your fruits to grow. He wants you to be empowered to leave the shore and do great things and in turn, teach your children to leave the shore and seek the adventure that He has in store for them.

Something else that little children are famous for is that they get homesick. As great as camp is, or as exciting as it is to go to college, sailing away from shore is exhilarating, but it is always comforting to go back home. God sent you out in this big beautiful world and He has plans for you, but He wants you to come home one day. Homesickness ... a desire to come home. We don't belong in this world, you see this world isn't our home. We are on a journey and just traveling through this foreign land. We aren't an heir to the throne here on earth but called to a heavenly kingdom where we are heirs to the King. God tells us that there is a promise of a room waiting for us in heaven. The Bible tells us over and over again that

God created you, He loves you, He wants you to do great things on your journey but eventually He wants you to come home. He will be waiting with the light on.

As we develop a relationship with God and begin to allow Him to be our heavenly Father, then we can start acting like His children. To be empowered by knowing what His promises are and to have a life transformed by those promises. To feel His peace in all circumstances and to have a clear knowledge of the direction that we are traveling. We will have an opportunity to develop wisdom and to grow the Fruit of the Spirit.

Parenting is the toughest job you will ever experience. The sooner that you call out for help the sooner that God will ride "shotgun" with you. He will be on the seat next to you for the drive. I once traveled into New York City with a group of friends pre-GPS and my girlfriend who was riding shotgun had the first MapQuest directions I had ever seen. As we emerged from the Lincoln Tunnel she was able to direct me block by block which lane to be in and when a turn was coming. I was so nervous before the trip about driving in the city but once Julie took charge and directed me, my sweaty palms ceased and I felt 100 percent better. I could relax, knowing that she was guiding me and telling me which lane to be in and how many blocks we needed to travel. That is what I feel like when I have God riding shotgun with me. I still have to make the journey, but step by step I have God directing my path and telling me where to go. How do I know where God wants me to go and what He wants me to do? By talking to Him regularly and trusting that if something is His will for me things will fall into place. If I keep hitting roadblocks then it probably isn't His will or timing. When something feels heavy on my heart like visiting someone, I make an effort to go. I can't tell you the number of times that I see God's hand in the action, for the person really needed some support or they were hurting and needed the love of a friend. If I feel anxious then I know that in some way I have left God's path and I need to find a way to get back on track.

On my children's behalf, I pray constantly for them. I pray for their friends and I pray for their future spouse. I pray over their teachers and their coaches. I pray daily for God to be with them and I encourage them to seek God's wisdom. If I sense darkness surrounding them, I pray aloud by the name of Jesus, for Satan to stay away from my child. You see God knows everything about me and He knows what is in my heart. I can pray silently and He hears me clearly but Satan can only judge me by my actions and my words. If I feel evil around me, my family or my community I pray aloud for Satan to leave those I love alone. And I do it by calling out the name of Jesus. Scripture tells us that that there is power in the name of Jesus. I know that He is stronger than me so I feel confident in calling out His name and letting Him fight the battle that I am unable to do on my own.

The little shepherd boy David did just that when he confronted the giant Goliath with nothing more than a slingshot and a stone. He called out the name of God and God directed the path of that stone to hit its mark. He will do the same for you each and every time you ask. But it does require faith. The impossible can be transformed by a simple act of faith. Jesus tells us that all we need is faith the size of a mustard seed to engage His power. Then He will move mountains for you. He will heal a broken heart, give strength to those suffering addiction, bring comfort to those who mourn, and bring peace to those who are ill. There is no limit to what God can do and the great thing is you don't have to earn it. The Bible is a who's who of sinners who reached out to God and He did great things in their lives. When you humbly get down on your knees, unbelievable things can happen. Find comfort in His presence and peace will flow, fruit will grow, and love will flourish.

Because you are older and wiser than your child, you have much to teach them. God has entrusted your children to your care and your child desperately need to hear from you what you value and what you feel is important. We live in a world where far too many parents have outsourced the job of raising their children and the results have proved costly. Make no mistake, your child is going to learn about life from somebody, and if you aren't willing to step up to the plate someone else will. Be aware that they are learning about life every single day. Some of the lessons are positive but many of them aren't. So you need to ask yourself the question, "Is my child being tutored by the world or by me?

To help you on this journey I put together a letter of lessons that I wanted to be sure that my children knew. These are 20 things that I wanted to tell my kids before they left home. I'm sure that you can add to the list but it may serve as a guide of things that you want them to pack in their bags before they embark on their road to independence.

To my Dear Child,

Here is a list of things that I want you to know before you say goodbye to life in our home and start the next chapter on your own.

1. God's Plan ... God has a plan for your life that's bigger and better, than yours.
2. Faith ... With faith you can move mountains, without faith you can't.
3. Doing what's right ... It's more important to be right than to be popular.
4. Work ... Hard work pays tremendous dividends, so the time to get busy is now. (Pray as if everything depended upon God, but work as if everything depended upon you)
5. Time Management ... Life is shorter than you think, so make every day count.
6. Optimism pays, pessimism doesn't. Trust your hopes, not your fears.
7. Opportunities are everywhere, so keep your eyes and heart open.
8. Safety ... It's more dangerous out there than you think, so play safe and don't be impulsive. (Maturity and safety go hand in hand)

9. Character ... The sooner you learn that character really matters, the sooner you'll earn the respect of your peers and yourself. (Character is what you are when nobody is watching.)

10. Celebrate life the right way ... If you don't celebrate life, nobody's going to celebrate it for you. (Today, like every other day, is a cause for celebration. God gives us this day; He fills it to the brim with possibilities, and He challenges us to use it for His purposes.)

11. Regret ... You can't win them all; don't waste time regretting the ones you lose.

12. Service ... It is important to serve others and develop an attitude of selflessness where you learn to see others needs.

13. Humility ... Since pride usually precedes a fall, stay humble (God honors humility, and He rewards those who humbly serve Him.)

14. Kindness ... It pays to be respectful, so treat everyone like you want to be treated if you were in their shoes.

15. Being healthy ... Take care of your body; it's the only one you've got.

16. Peer pressure ... Since you'll inevitably become more like your friends, choose your friends wisely. (Find people who bring out the best in you.)

17. Prayer ... Prayer is more powerful than you think, so if you need something, ask God. (The quality of your child's life will be in direct proportion to the quality of their prayer life. Prayer changes things and it will change them)

18. Maintaining proper perspective ... as you grow older, things will happen that you simply cannot understand unless you remember that God has an eternal perspective. (Psalm 46:10 Be still, and know that I am God.)

19. Temptations ... Remain vigilant, temptations are everywhere ... Don't be alarmed, expect it.

20. Eternal Life ... Nothing is more important than knowing the way to get home. Always remember that you have the

keys to the front door and that when that day comes God will be there welcoming you and saying "Well done my good and faithful servant."

Love, Mom and Dad xoxoxo

CHAPTER 14
Sending The Boats Out To Sea

~

To be loved is the greatest desire of the human heart. It is something that we all crave and spend a lifetime in pursuit of. Yet, another person can't fully satisfy this need, only God can... he designed people that way. Why would God create humanity with this deep need and never meet it?

That is a very interesting thought. I believe that He made us this way so that we all have an inner desire to fulfill ourselves spiritually. Even people who claim that they don't need God have a sense that something is missing. They spend a lifetime trying to fill that void with things or accomplishments yet it never seems to completely satisfy. It's amazing how many people I know who live a very simple life, yet their faith is so strong that they live their lives as if they are the wealthiest people on the earth. Their cup is full and they pour out that cup on others. You've seen them, people who just give of themselves because they couldn't think of doing anything less. Yet, there are others who have wealth and goods to satisfy themselves ten times over, yet they hoard these gifts and as a result tend to be miserable. What makes the difference?

There was a story of a man who bought himself a Cadillac. He loved his car and all that it represented. One day he went to visit a friend who didn't have a driveway and as a result he had to park his new car in the roadway. All during lunch the man kept looking out the window, checking on his car to be sure it was okay. Finally, well before they enjoyed their entire visit the man decided to leave. He was too anxious and distracted about his car that he couldn't focus on anything else. The friend realized that his friend didn't own a Cadillac, the Cadillac owned the friend.

The danger that occurs when we attach too much importance to things over people is that things never completely satisfy. Pursuit of material objects rob us of our peace and detaches us from seeing clearly the needs of others. We are always coveting what someone else has and therefore our eyes are deceived. We lose our peace and our ability to see to the needs of others. As parents, we may have a need to supply our children with everything they want. A new bike, the latest phone, a nice car, etc. but what our children really need is our love. A sense that they are valued and that their home is a safe place. When they have that reassurance, they can feel confident to venture away from the shore.

One of the most loving gesture that a parent can make is to let their child leave the safety of the shore and travel away from home. It can also be the most frightening. As we prepare our children for their journey, we want to empower them with the security that comes from knowing that they are loved. When our children leave home I'm sure most of them hear the words of their parents: "Be careful, call if you need anything, make wise choices, stay out of trouble." God gives us that same message when He sends His children out into a hostile world. We may not physically hear the words but it is part of our makeup ... to have a spiritual desire that we long to fill. That is why people, places, and things can never completely satisfy this need. He knew that we would need reassurance, so He gave us His words in the form of the Bible. For centuries, the Bible has provided wisdom, comfort and guidance to God's children.

As we prepare to send our little boat out to sea with our priceless children on board we want to be sure that we are sending them out there with a clear understanding who they are. They don't belong to this world but they are heirs to the throne of the heavenly kingdom of God. Do they know this? They are embarking on a journey that will take them far from home in body, mind, and spirit and we need to ask ourselves, do they have the tools required for this separation? Do they know how to get to the final destination? Do they know where that destination is?

Many of the lessons in this book keep repeating themselves. I will say the same thing in chapter two and then repeat it again in chapter ten. The reason for this is to drive the simple but important messages home. It really isn't that complicated but it needs to be reinforced often. God wants a relationship with you, He loves you, He sent His Spirit to help you on your journey, and He gave us a roadmap on how to find our way home. The only question is; will you say yes to His help and guidance or do you want to travel by yourself?

Each child grows at different rates and each of our children will mature when the timing is right for them. With that in mind there are certain stages that each child will go through that have key elements on timing.

I teach Newborn Classes at a very large Medical Center. We deliver almost 7,000 babies a year and besides having been the head nurse on one of the post partum units I am a maternal/child educator. My goal, plain and simple, is to reduce the anxiety level of the new parents. I want to help them have the tools that they will need to care for this precious little baby (who unfortunately doesn't come with instructions). They are very anxious, especially if they haven't had much exposure with babies, and my job is to try to break through this anxiety layer and help them retain the most important information.

This chapter will be a review of the big ticket items that you need to focus on before you send your child out the door on their own. The more you empower your child, the more successful they will be. Both the educated and the uneducated may experience the same issues but the person who has the tools, and knows how to cope, will be able to be successful without a lot of stress and anxiety.

They will know what to look for and how to spot dangers along the way. As a result, they will have the gift of peace along the journey.

BODY

As I mentioned before, your job as a new parent will be to try to figure out who this little person is? Are they a guzzler, or a nibbler when they are hungry? Do they wake up after a bath (give the bath during the day) or does the bath knock them out (give the bath just before bed)? These are observations that new parents will need to make and as a result they can change their behavior. There are lots of things to teach the new parents but the one thing that they have to get right is the baby's hydration. The baby is too little to get this one wrong. It really doesn't matter how often or when you give a bath or if they sleep through the night (although it would be nice if they came with that desire). What matters is that are they hydrated and growing, especially a low birth weight baby. How do you check that? An experienced or educated parent may know to check the baby's output, how many wet diapers they are producing (what goes in, must come out). But an inexperienced parent may not be aware that they need to check the baby's output. You can also check the baby's skin turgor. If you pinch the baby's skin does it immediately go back or does it stay pinched? An observation that I can make is that most of our senior citizen population is dehydrated. If you pinched their skin it would stay pinched. That is because they don't drink enough fluids (mostly because they don't want to keep having to go to the bathroom). As a result they don't process their medicines as well, they have trouble warding off infections and they may not think as clearly. All of these things can be helped with a simple glass of water. In a baby's world you are in charge of what they drink and their hydration level so new parents need tools to assess if this need is being met. Besides those two observations that I mentioned there is another wonderful way to assess if the baby is well hydrated and that is to check the fontanelle. What exactly is that? A newborn's skull is made up of plates that overlap to allow the baby's passage through the birth canal. Once the baby is born you will notice that they have two fontanelles or *soft spots* on the top and back of their head. These will ossify over time but initially they are a wonderful indicator to let us know if the baby is dehydrated. If the fontanelle sinks in, it can alert us to the possibility that the baby isn't taking in enough fluids, if it it soft and flat we can be comforted in knowing that they are well hydrated. Armed with this bit of knowledge allows a parent to make assessments on the baby's health and well being and as a result they can rest.

My goal as an educator is to be sure that new parents have the tools and understanding to help them during labor and afterward when caring for their baby. I try to keep things as simple as possible and I use lots of word pictures that will help them to understand and retain the information.

Word pictures are nothing more than stories that will help, not only get the information across but be retained. When talking about bringing the baby home I stress the importance of new moms taking care of themselves. The example that I give is that on a plane they tell you if the oxygen mask comes down, you should put it on yourself first, and then you help your child. Likewise, new moms need to take care of themselves so that they are able to care for their little one. It isn't a good situation if mom is exhausted and then has to do the new twenty-four-hour, seven-day-a- week job of being a mother. If they are nursing, they need to have a drink beside them to replenish their own fluids; if the baby naps, they should nap because if the baby is up they will be up, or the idea to wear lounging pajamas when they first get home from the hospital to remind themselves that they are still a patient themselves, even though they are home. By telling the story of the oxygen mask it may help a mom remember to take care of herself and not feel guilty about it. Let's face it, parenthood is a constant struggle about guilt and new parents need to learn early that they won't be a perfect parent but it certainly helps to take care of themselves so that they can be the best parent possible.

As we help our children grow, there are many lessons that we will need to teach them, some are vital and some are just helpful. Some can be taught when they are small and others have specific timing. The goal is to help your child to have the tools that they will need as they get ready to set out on their own. You can't wait until they are packing their bags to go off to college before you teach these things but they must marinate over time so they become part of your child's fabric.

Have you educated them on the changes that their body will go through? Do they know how to eat properly and what a balanced diet looks like? Do they understand the need to be physically active? Do they know how to control their moods? A child needs to learn how to care for themselves and how to manage this body of theirs. My daughter-in-law had a wonderful way to teach her three-year-old how to calm down when he was upset with his brother. She had him put up his three fingers to represent his age and one by one he needed to blow out his candles. She taught him how to regroup and then he was able to tell her what was wrong. What about manners? Do they know how to sit properly and behave at the dinner table and a restaurant? Can they interact with adults and know how to address their grandparents, teachers, police, and coaches with respect?

There are many lessons that you will need to teach your children and the best way to teach these lessons is with modeling them yourself. By cultivating a home of HONOR and RESPECT and spending time taking care of yourself, it allows you to have the energy and wisdom to be able to instruct these precious little people that God entrusted to your care.

I put together a sample list of the items that I thought was important to teach my children before they flew the nest. Your list may be different and it can certainly be added upon but it is something to think about so that you aren't left scrambling as they pack their bags and prepare to push off the shore.

1. How to set a table (Fork is 4 letters, left is 4 letters; right, spoon and knife are all 5 letters)
2. How to prepare some meals

3. How to be sure the meals are balanced (A colorful plate)
4. Changes in their bodies (Go shopping together for needed supplies when they turn 10 years old. Items to include: deodorant, nail clippers, face wash, sanitary pads for girls, etc.)
5. How to be responsible with their body (Good things in, good things out ... bad things in, bad things out)
6. How to do some chores around the house
7. How to do their own laundry
8. How to be prepared in the morning for school
9. How to be prepared for their extracurricular activities
10. How to bring balance to their lives (Having some down time)
11. How to change a tire and jump start a car
12. How to repair something if they broke it
13. How to navigate a grocery store
14. How to write a thank you letter
15. How to buy thoughtful gifts for other people
16. How to balance their finances

These are just some ideas that you may want to teach your child before they leave home. It take time to teach life lessons, so you want to be sure that you allow enough time and allow them to marinate into who they are.

MIND

Who is your child on the inside? How do they handle conflict? Are they in control of their emotions? Are they an extrovert or an introvert? All questions that give us an idea of who this person is.

My oldest son was my "most everything." Every emotion that he had, he experienced with a passion. He was my most affectionate, and my most angry. He was passionate about sports and not so passionate about school. He was outgoing and opinionated. He had lots of friends that were over our house **a lot,** and some of them even lived with us for a time. He was the most attentive to his grandparents and even cared for his grandmother for a year and a half after her husband of 62 years died.

My daughter, on the other hand was balanced and calm. She kept things to herself and didn't play her cards far from her chest. She quietly did her work and was tremendously responsible. She was kind to everyone but valued her few true friends above all. Even as early as Kindergarten she was independent. She liked doing things her own way and valued time organizing her room, something my son would never have thought was important.

How did I grow such totally opposite children? And how was I to raise them to enhance their individual strengths? It was a challenge and I needed tools to help me do my job. Add to that two additional priceless children and I realized that I couldn't do it on my own.

What did I do? I became a student of my children and with that I educated myself on child rearing. I bought books that helped me (there are a lot of great parenting books out there). I attended a parenting group and I became a member of a babysitting co-op. These were tools that I used, especially in the early days, to help me gain wisdom. It also allowed me a place to vent, explore options, and hear from other mothers about their experiences. It was especially helpful to hear from moms whose kids were a stage or two ahead of mine to educate me on what was coming so that I was prepared.

I became involved in my children's school so that I knew the teachers and, more important, that they knew me. They could help me gain insight into who my child was and tell me if their behavior was appropriate. I became aware of the difference between a developmental stage and a character flaw. I learned to be aware of what behavior was a problem and what behavior I could let slide. I was involved in the PTA and scouting programs. I volunteered to be the team parent with their sports teams and was the room mom for their classrooms.

How do you find time to read, educate, and attend ... you make it your priority. Yes, it is easier to relax on the couch after a long day, but spending time gaining wisdom is so vital to the wellbeing of your home especially in the years of turbulent waters. Energy spent today will help you gain wisdom and insight into your child and may be the key to help your child navigate those dangerous waters.

"The mind is a dangerous thing to waste" was a slogan for the commercial to support the United Negro College Fund. I still remember that slogan because it meant something. It struck a chord with me that I wasn't going to allow my children to waste their minds. I didn't want them to waste the gifts that God empowered them with and my job was to cultivate that gift as best I could. That meant that I wouldn't allow my children to be lazy. Oh they could have low-key days and as a matter of fact, I encouraged it at times. But I was holding them responsible for their lives. That meant that I was on top of them to complete their homework. I spent time going to back to school night so I could meet their teachers and learn what their expectations were. I was able to learn what they were going to be teaching so I could engage my children about what they were learning. My one son's teacher even sent home an extra copy of the book they were reading in high school so that I could read along with him. It gave me the opportunity to read some great books but also an opportunity to have a discussion at the dinner table about the book he was reading.

I had a son who had comprehension issues when he read silently, so I put in the effort of reading his history book aloud to him. His comprehension improved significantly. This required "being there" for him and believe me it was exhausting but 100 percent worth it. Today my children are successful and happy with their career choices. I have a doctor, and engineer, a principal with his PHD and a president of a Foundation. I gave them the tools so that they could fly.

What that meant for me was some great time-management lessons. I decided to not volunteer for anything that took me away from the home at night that didn't benefit me or my children. I could do activities during the day while they were at school but in the evening, my kids needed me and I preciously guarded that time. I knew that the first 15 minutes when my children came in the door from school was vital. They had stories to tell and problems to solve. It wasn't a time to begin talking about homework or the chores they didn't do. That would come, but when they immediately came in the door, I asked them what they wanted to eat and I paused with them. Those 15 minutes made all the difference. They allowed us to connect and regroup. When four kids walk in the door at the same time it can be quite a scene and I can remember how much I liked it when they were in different schools or activities and I was able to greet them one at a time. Spending just a short time with each of them at key moments will then free you up to attend to your needs. Once they tell their stories they are off either playing or tending to their school work and you aren't needed as much. It sets the tone for the rest of the evening.

I did make sure that I carved in time for just me, whether with my girlfriends, participating in sports or on dates with my husband, I knew that I needed that "me time" to help me feel fulfilled. Balance is something that I needed to model for my kids so that they could see its value in their own lives.

Parenting is a full-time and exhausting job, but one the the greatest jobs that you will ever have. To be given the responsibility to care, cultivate, and grow another human being is an awesome responsibility. Try not to get overwhelmed or burned out but try to find balance and the ability to see the joy along the way.

Some things to give some thought to as you look to cultivate their minds:

1. Notice them ... so you can notice changes in their behavior.
2. Listen to them ... they will value themselves and their voice if they feel that they are being heard.
3. Set boundaries ... let them know where the fences are.
4. Be honest ... let them know that they can trust you.
5. Delight in their discoveries and accomplishments ... look for opportunities to expand their minds.
6. Know what their dreams are ... where do you see their talents?

7. Establish traditions … it forges memories and things they can count on.
8. Be there … show up at games and concerts.
9. Have fun … life is short, learn to keep some things light.
10. Tell them about your growing-up years and your fears and dreams.
11. Praise more and criticize less.
12. Be consistent … they notice.
13. Admit when you make a mistake and help them learn from theirs.
14. Pamper them … don't spoil them but occasionally indulge in a treat.
15. Be flexible … it teaches them to know how to deal with changing winds.
16. Ask them to help you … a family is a team sport.
17. Feed them good food, good words, and good role models (help them to be people of excellence).
18. Let them make mistakes …we all make them.
19. Give them good choices … let them be wisdom seekers.
20. Become their advocate … let them know that you are in their court.
21. Accept who they are … remember we are all unique.
22. Encourage them to help others … teach them kindness.
23. Tell them what you expect of them … they need to be held accountable.
24. Expose them to new things … let life be a lifetime journey of learning.
25. Expect their best but don't expect perfection … encourage them to try.
26. Encourage them to do it themselves … independence builds confidence.
27. Encourage them to spend time with the grandparents … it cultivates family connections and helps them to value the wisdom that comes with age.

SPIRIT

Nothing is more important than spending time cultivating your children's faith. Life is hard and the road is long. There are dangers and detours that can cause grave consequences if your child isn't on guard. By helping them depend on God you allow them to have wise council all along the way. That is a tremendous comfort when they leave the shore and travel beyond the horizon. When they are out of your sight who will they turn to when the seas get rough? By spending time in their early years cultivating a relationship with their Heavenly Father they will know with confidence that they aren't alone in their boat. They will know that they can call out and God will bring them peace in the midst of the storm.

This is a loud and challenging world and it is hard to hear God's voice when the storms are raging all around us. How do you teach your children and yourself who God is and what are His promises to His children? It occurs by spending time in His presence when the storms aren't raging and the waters are calm. It requires you to be a student of His word and have an understanding of His desire to have a relationship with all of His children.

It is a challenge to intimately know God when there is so much noise and conflicting information coming at you about who God is and what God's will is. You have imperfect people telling you what you should believe and then their actions don't match what they preach. How do you develop an understanding about God that allows you to have confidence in what you believe?

There is a story about a man who became an expert on detecting counterfeit bills. He had a 100 percent success rate in picking out the true money from the false. It may seem very overwhelming to have to be on constant guard for new ways to copy money so that you can detect what is true and what is false but he had as system that allowed him to be correct every time.

If you wanted to be an expert in detecting counterfeit bills, how would you do it? Would you spend time examining all the ways that people print money that pass as true bills? That would be exhausting and probably not effective because people would come up with new ways all the time to cheat the system. The way to become an expert is to know what the true bill looks and feels like. If you know the real bill , then it will allow you to detect the counterfeit.

Having a relationship with God is like that. When you know what the real God is like, what His promises are and how much He loves you, then you can detect if something isn't from God. When His peace is missing in your life then you know that what you are doing or feeling isn't from God. He will bring you peace during the storms and it is as simple as calling out to Him. It takes time to learn to trust Him and hide His word in your heart but when you have an understanding of the "real" God then you can learn to rest in His presence when the world gets crazy.

God tells us that He knows that this journey is hard, He sent His son on the same journey to educate us on the way to get home. He also sent us a helper in the form of the Holy Spirit. A helper who lives within us to guide us on our journey. God knew we were going to need protection and that we would need to guard our hearts from the dangers that surround us.

Because the journey is hard, God equips us with His armor to protect us. The armor of God can be found in **Ephesians 6:10-18.**

The Armor of God
10 Finally, be strong in the Lord and in his mighty power. 11 Put on the full armor of God, so that you can take your stand against the devil's schemes. 12 For our struggle is not against flesh and blood, but against the rulers, against the authorities, against the powers of this dark world and against the spiritual forces of evil in the heavenly realms. 13 Therefore put on the full armor of God, so that when the day of evil comes, you may be able to stand your ground, and after you have done everything, to stand. 14 Stand firm then, with the belt of truth buckled around your waist, with the breastplate of righteousness in place, 15 and with your feet fitted with the readiness that comes from the gospel of peace. 16 In addition

*to all this, take up the shield of faith, with which you can
extinguish all the flaming arrows of the evil one. 17 Take the
helmet of salvation and the sword of the Spirit, which is the
word of God.*
*18 And pray in the Spirit on all occasions with all kinds of
prayers and requests. With this in mind, be alert and always
keep on praying for all the Lord's people.*

What exactly does that mean, and what does it mean for our
spouse and children? It means to be ready for battle ... DAILY!
The world is challenging and we need to be prepared to meet those
challenges. You wouldn't send your child out to sea without training,
guidance, or protection, so why would you send them out into the
world without those same tools? Paul tells us in Ephesians that you
are going into battle but God has provided His armor to protect you.

The Belt of Truth ... This vital piece of the armor supports your
core and holds all of the important and vital tools. By knowing
God's truths it allows you to stand tall in the face of adversity. The
truth is that God created you, loves you, sent you here with a free
will to choose if you want to be in His family but ultimately, He
wants you to come home. These are His promises.

Breastplate of Righteousness ... This covers your heart with
His protection so that you become a person of character. The breastplate protects your heart from burning arrows that may be sent your
way. The arrows may be attacks on your beliefs, or your peace. By
having a breastplate you can ward off those attacks and not allow
your heart to be wounded. You are right with God because you hear
His voice and read His word.

Shield of Faith ... Arrows of doubt, worry, and anxiety are
being shot at you daily. By using your shield to ward off concerns
it allows you to grow in knowing God by seeing that He keeps His
promises. He can be trusted.

The Helmet of Salvation ... It helps you to know whose team
you are on. You belong to God and are an heir to the throne. Stand

proudly in this knowledge and know that your team already won the battle. You are guaranteed everlasting life.

Feet Fitted with Readiness ... You wouldn't enter battle barefoot, therefore it is important that you are ready at a moment's notice to go to battle. The battle may be to witness who God is to your children or a friend. It may be that you received news that you have cancer and need to face that evil head on, or maybe death struck your family and your faith is being put to the test. Have your shoes ready at a moments notice for you don't know when the call will come that you need to stand tall and face your enemy.

All of these pieces of armor are to protect you. They offer you cover against the enemy and keep you safe. But the final piece of the armor is the only piece that is offensive.

The Sword of the Spirit ... This is the word of God. This is your steel to fight the enemy. It is vital that you keep it sharp. How do you keep it sharp? By hiding God's word in your heart so that it is ready when you need it. Spend time getting to know Him by reading His words. Memorize key scripture that can bring you comfort in times of need. Know His promises, so that you can ward off doubt when it appears. Attend a Bible study so that you can know and understand Him and His desire for your life. Cultivate this in your children. I do sword drills in my Confirmation classes where I call out a scripture passage and the first one who finds it gets a piece of candy. I might say John 3:16 and the kids race to be the first to find it in their Bible. I want them comfortable in God's word, the Holy Bible.

Knowing about God's armor is a wonderful lesson to teach your children, and for you to learn yourself. God wants you to have a successful journey and the sooner that you understand that you can't do it on your own, the better your life will be. He doesn't want you unprotected out in this world but He wants you empowered with His armor so that you can be safe even during the battles that you will face. Parenting is the toughest job you'll ever experience and there will be battles that you will encounter but having your armor on daily will allow you to face those battles head-on and come out the other side successfully. You will have wisdom and confidence as you face enemies and then you will be able to be a witness for God to your children. You can then empower them with the same armor that kept you safe and guarded your heart. You can live a life of peace and have confidence in the direction that you are traveling because you have God by your side. Let God ride "shotgun" ... He knows the way home!

Helping your child grow in faith and wisdom empowers them to make wise decisions that help them grow into Godly people. It allows them to thank God in all circumstances even the challenging ones. Faith is like the wind, you can't see the wind but you can see the effects. As you cultivate God in your life you will see its impact and so will others around you. You will feel God's peace even during the storms, you will experience self-control even when the house is full of chaos and you will love even when someone behaves poorly. Don't you want your kids to experience that same power?

Your home life will be transformed as your family *walks worthily*, in all situations, because they know that they belong to royalty. If you are a child of a king you don't want to eat garbage when you know a feast is awaiting. Build your house on a rock and trust that when the floods and winds come, the foundation will hold. You will receive God's blessing in all situations, and learn to trust even when the outcome isn't what you wanted, but believe that God has a plan that is right for you. When you truly ask God to be your Father you can rest knowing that He has your best interest at heart. It is then that you can pour out your blessings on others and help them to grow.

CHAPTER 15

What Happens After The Ship Sails

I am at a point in my life when I get to enjoy the fruits of my labor. My children are all grown and they have been successful in their career paths, married spouses who truly bring out the best in them and they are at a point where we are welcoming the next generation into our home. I delight in watching them sail on and gain control of their lives, especially after watching them travel through the challenging waters of their teenage years.

I learned long ago that most of parenting required attentive eyes, a strong desire to get the truth, and a lot of "tweaking." Only rarely did I feel the need to get my guns loaded and address a problem with full force. Most of the time it was assessing the situation and asking God for wisdom in addressing the issue. Usually, it was God giving me a sense of calm and challenging me to not overreact. It took some time for me to reach that wisdom. I developed an attitude that there would be consequences for their actions and tried to stop all the nagging that I found myself doing. I tried to take myself out of the equation and not allow *me* to be the problem. Plus, I was tired of hearing myself talk.

"If this, then that ..." became my new formula.

If homework isn't done, **then** you can't participate in your team's practice until it is. I wasn't going to allow them to let the team down as that was a responsibility that they signed up for. It meant that I took them to practice and they sat in the bleachers doing their homework until it was done. Then they could join the team in their practice.

Likewise, being part of a team required them to be responsible. That meant that it was their responsibility to be prepared for practice or a game. I wasn't responsible for their uniform being cleaned and getting their gear ready. If they were old enough to play, they were old enough to be prepared. I wasn't going to be sitting in the car waiting for them but they needed to be in the car waiting for me. We had the discussion about what their responsibility was before we signed them up. After a few seasons of stress and anxiety before a game or practice we developed a new code. Responsibility. An understanding about what was expected from them.

The same is true with chores, *"If* your room is clean, *then* you can have a friend over." *"If* you set the table, *then* we will eat." *"If* you speak disrespectfully to me, *then* you can't go out with your friends." Consequences were clear and understood.

Eventually, I was successful in teaching my child to be an independent, self-sufficient adult. When I look back, I realized that for a time, I wasn't allowing my children to learn from their actions. I needed to educate them on what was expected and what the consequences were if those expectations weren't met. My oldest son's greatest fear in life when he was in junior high school, was that he would read a chapter that wasn't required. He was always looking for the easy way out. Today he has his doctorate in education and is a principal of a middle school. I couldn't be more proud of the young man he became but I believe it started when I finally let him sail his own boat.

As you start to see with clarity what your true role as a parent is ... to help them be independent ... then you are able to see the big picture. You can discern if your actions are helping or hindering in that process.

There is a story about a little boy who was having trouble putting a puzzle together. He calls out to his father, "Daddy, can you help me?" The father quickly assembles the puzzle and the little boy responds, "Daddy, how could you do that so fast?" The father replies, "Son, when you put the puzzle together you looked at the pieces, but when I put it together, I looked at the whole picture."

You see, the goal isn't to assemble the puzzle for our kids. Our goal is to be the great encourager and help them to put the puzzle together for themselves. It may seem so obvious to us that the purple piece doesn't belong where the green pieces are forming grass or that the flat sided piece doesn't belong in the middle of the puzzle. Many times it is easier to just assemble the puzzle for them but that isn't the goal. We need to encourage them to become wise and see how the big picture will look.

I am sure I speak for most parents who dedicated themselves to their children, that there is a certain joy that comes when your kids pass through those turbulent waters of the teenage years and they find safe passage out to sea and begin their journey away from your guiding light.

Now what?

That is the question that many parents ask themselves when their children travel on and leave your home. They may stay close by or they may travel to another state or even another country. They are headed for the open seas and our job is not as vital as it once was. We don't need to constantly be on the lookout for them and worry if they have the skills to navigate the challenging waters. We empowered them with the tools they would need to leave the safety of the harbor and sail beyond the sight of land.

We now have an empty nest and we have to reassess what our purpose is and readjust to a new role. What do we do for ourselves that allows us to find purpose and keep our light burning? That is the challenge.

I think the first area that needs to be addressed is our focus. What was once 110 percent on our kids has now shifted to our spouse. In many cases we have both grown in different areas and when we have the time to refocus on our relationship we don't recognize each other. Our conversation used to revolve around what the kids were doing and how to handle situations in their lives. We used to have interactions with friends that we met because of our children, the people we saw on the bleachers or auditoriums of our kids' journeys. We may suddenly find ourselves with little to talk about. We miss the ease of friendships that just happened because we sat next to each other on a cold rainy day watching our kids play.

This is a real adjustment, as our world has now changed from being a lifesaving role with our focus on raising our children to a maintenance role of just being sure that things are moving along smoothly.

Another observation is what is our role in our children's lives? They don't seek our counsel as often as they use to and they now have other resources to go to for that counsel. A professor, friends, a steady relationship all play an important part in their new lives away from the safe harbor from home. Eventually, we may have to share them with their in-laws. This may mean the change from celebrating Christmas the "way we always do" to celebrating Christmas a week before the 25th, because they are going to the in-laws' on Christmas Day.

I speak for myself and many of my friends when I write this chapter. After twenty-plus years in an exhausting, satisfying, thankless, rewarding job, how do you retire? How do we navigate this next chapter?

First... Let it be a chapter of self-discovery. We just spent twenty-plus years with our focus on our family, now it is time to focus on ourselves a bit. I have a little sign in my kitchen that says;

"Who were you before you put yourself last?"

Who are you? What brings you joy?

Did you always want to be an artist? Sign up for an art class. Did you want to cultivate your faith? Find a Bible study (look beyond your own church doors if needed.) If that isn't successful, either begin a journey of reading the Bible yourself or start your own small group Bible study. There are lots of great resources that can help guide you on this journey. Did you want to get in shape? Join a gym or find some friends to walk with. Take up a new sport such as golf, tennis, or maybe sailing. It feels great to play again. Many of us no longer see our bank accounts draining as they did when we supported our kids, so use that money in support of your interests and hobbies. If the funds aren't there, then look for free avenues to cultivate a new interest. Join a book club, or take a free class that the library offers. Join a community club like the women's club or the seniors. Volunteer at the local food shelter, your church, or library. Teach a Sunday school class. Nothing keeps you going like being around kids, especially now that you have a lot more patience and time.

I teach Confirmation to the seventh-and eighth-graders from our church and I just love this age because they are usually such a mess! They are trying to go through that transition between childhood and adulthood and I like to think that I am a calm place for them to rest for an hour and a half every other week. I get a kick out of them and they know it. I have been doing this for over twenty years and I can't recall a child ever being disrespectful to me, mostly because I try not to be disrespectful to them. That can only happen if you are at a place of peace.

Peace ... I love that word. The Bible tells us 365 times to not be anxious, to be at peace. That means daily, we are to put our trust in Him and receive His peace as an answer.

This is the time in our lives when we should enjoy the fruits of our labors. The ability to see what a lifetime of trials, joys, and challenges cultivated in our lives. We have poured our heart and soul into something and now we get to sit back and watch what we cultivated. Pause for a moment and reflect back on your own individual journey away from the safety of the harbor. You may remember how your parents wanted you home for dinner when you came back from a break at college and how you craved spending time with your friends and couldn't wait to reconnect with them. Your sight was looking out and your parents' longing was to call you home to be sure you were okay and properly equipped for the journey. Try to keep that in mind with your own kids. Try not to take it personally when they would rather spend time with their high school classmates than sitting in your living room. They may have stories to share but it might not be with you and your spouse. This can be hurtful, but remember, your goal was to make them independent, self-sufficient, responsible adults. If you did your job properly, then they trust that you will be there for them if they need anything. They have the confidence in your love and support so they don't need that reassurance, it's already there. Once the excitement of their first journey out to sea is over, their world will balance out and you will see them become more stable in their boats and navigate the pull between family and friends.

This is also a time in your child's life when they are preparing to find a life mate. I will speak about your marriage in a moment but first it is important to help your child understand what picking a life mate means. To find someone who brings out the best in you and with whom you can trust. There is a story about a young woman who bought a tie that she liked, before she went away to college. She left it on her bedpost in her dorm and used it as a reminder to pray for her future husband. For seven years it hung on her bedpost or on the dresser mirror and she said it reminded her more times than she could count to pray that God would encourage, grow and spiritually develop her someday husband into the man of God she desired. On the eve of her wedding she presented the tie to her future husband. The next day he stood at the alter with his hand over the tie and tears in his eyes. God was faithful!

MARRIAGE

Marriage is nothing more than two imperfect people sharing a journey together. As you travel, you may notice that after awhile you both get worn down a bit. An observation that I have is that many of our quirks and habits become more pronounced at this chapter of our lives. We may become more opinionated, inflexible, or gossipy. Those are the cobwebs that I want to keep out of my lighthouse. It is vital for our overall health to do frequent inspections and see where we need a bit of cleaning or repair work.

Perhaps our marriage has been neglected or we have allowed that part of our life to crumble completely. Maybe the spouse who we thought would be there for a lifetime is no longer in the picture either due to divorce or death and we have to adjust to a new normal.

If we are dealing with a neglected marriage it is time to put it to prayer and ask God to give you wisdom and insight. Maybe our focus was taken away from our spouse for so long that they have learned to function without us. Maybe we don't have as much in common as we used to. Maybe our mutual, comfortable friends have split up or moved away and left us feeling like two strangers who just have each other.

So what exactly is marriage?

Marriage is picking someone for the life journey. Someone who agreed to join you on the highs and lows of this rollercoaster ride called life. I taught a marriage class and I began with the comment that you don't get married to be *happy*. That took one husband by surprise and he asked if I could please clarify that statement. I said that the reason you marry is share the journey, perhaps start a family, and build a life together with another person who is constantly rediscovering themselves. No one is happy when they are washing someone's underwear or cleaning the dishes. You married someone to share this journey with. You are an imperfect person, married to an imperfect person who raised a house of imperfect kids. Once you understand that, life can get a whole lot easier. It is time to "let go" of the expectation of perfection. It doesn't exist and don't forget if you expect a perfect spouse they may expect one in return!

"A God-honoring marriage is not created by finding a flawless spouse, but by allowing God's perfect love and acceptance to flow though an imperfect person (you) toward another imperfect person (your mate)."

It is never too late to rebuild and rediscover the relationship that brought you to this point on your journey. This is the time to reassess the conditions of your own boats and repair where some dry rot may have been discovered or where a new set of sails may be in order.

So what are the tools that you need to build a strong marriage? Just like having a blueprint is vital when building a house it is also necessary to have a plan when building your marriage.

The Foundation ... The base of your home. This sets up everything else that goes on top. If the foundation is out of kilter, the rest of the home may be in danger of collapse. Go to the root of your family and see if the foundation is stable. And what is the base of your home? Honor and Respect. Cultivating a home of honor and respect is vital for the well being of all of it's members. It is important to understand that the foundation needs to be on a level surface and that will be the key to everything that follows. If this vital step is missing then everything else can be out of kilter and won't be stable to support all the needs that follow. When we honor someone we are saying in effect that who they are and what they say carry great weight with us. They are valuable to us and as a result we choose to treat them with respect.

How do you honor someone? First and foremost you choose to. It is not something earned but something that we give unconditionally as an act of grace. People make a decision that they value something. Some people value jewels, others cars, and some put work at the top of their list of what they value. God is calling us to place Him at the top of your list of things you value and follow that with your spouse and family.

As you assess the foundation of your home you may need to do some good old attitude adjustments. Beginning today, you can readjust your attitude with the people that you share this journey with. It means giving your spouse a place of honor in your life. It means respecting the people who live in your home. When I first discovered this principle I realized that some of my actions were dishonoring to my husband. When he came home from a hard day at work I didn't greet him or make him feel valued but instead I had a list of demands for him as soon as he walked in the door. I didn't welcome him home and many times I didn't even have the outside lights on waiting for him. When you are expecting company you have the lights on to greet them as they arrived yet I didn't give my spouse that same consideration. Likewise, I needed to do that for my children as well. Being out in the world is a battlefield and the first thing I needed to do when they opened that door was to help them regroup and feel loved. Once I made the decision to change my behavior and greet my family when they arrived home my attitude toward them changed. I couldn't wait to welcome them home. I also realized something else, my behavior cost me two minutes. I turned on the lights and I got up when they came in the door. I valued them and as a result they felt loved. Our home was welcoming and safe.

I also made the decision to keep dishonoring actions at arm's length. We don't speak in disrespectful tones, we don't allow cursing in our home. We have our disagreements, but we have learned to fight fairly and to rise to a level of maturity instead of street fighting. I also tried to never embarrass my husband or kids, especially in front of others. I guarded my actions so that I didn't cheapen the value of my loved ones. If you have something you value like an antique dish passed down to you from your grandmother, you treat it with care. If you treat your cherished dish roughly it could chip or crack ... why then should I treat my loved one with less care? People make a decision that they value something or someone. What decision will you make about those around you?

Also, be kind with one another about whom we have become. We are a bit more weathered today then we were when we went through our 20's to 40's and we may need some loving attention to handle the markings of some challenging storms. Maybe some of our facade has cracked a bit and we certainly have a few more wrinkles, a few more pounds, and a few more scars. That gives us character and makes us unique. Hopefully you develop eyes to see the character in your spouse.

Honor is a decision that must be practiced daily and eventually it will become a vital part of your home. It will then flow down on your children and they will pass it on to the ones they love.

Think back to what attracted you to your spouse in the first place. What did you like about them? What were their dreams? What were your dreams? Were they achieved? Could they still be achieved? What new dreams can you develop.

Take some trips down memory lane. Maybe, go to the diner where you spent so many hours getting to know each other. Watch a movie that you enjoyed when you were dating. Take up a hobby that you used to do such as golf, skiing, or photography or find a new hobby to do together. Challenge yourselves to do one new thing each week. Going to a new restaurant, finding a new place to hike, or watching a new TV show are all things that can expand your world.

Travel together or with a group. Enjoy the planning and make sure that there is plenty of time to do what each of you like. My husband doesn't like cities and would much rather take an active trip. When we traveled to New York City we got tickets to a Broadway play but first we walked the entire Highline Trail (a recreational trail on the elevated railroad tracks in the center of the city). Compromise is a wonderful thing to learn. When traveling with our family of six I always tried to make sure I knew what everyone's number one thing to see or do was. Then I tried to make sure that we covered at least their number one or number two activity. It allowed them all to feel valued.

Reestablish a relationship at church if that fell to the wayside. You are entering into a world where you may need the support of a spiritual foundation as you change from the responsibility of caring for your children to maybe needing to care for and eventually lose your parents. Being part of a faith community can help during the trying times of caring for your parents and assisting them as they may loose their spouse or their independence.

Communication is also an area that needs to be rediscovered. Let's face it, we have heard all of our spouses stories so many times that you can run out of things to say. A healthy quiet isn't always a bad thing, as long as it doesn't lead to isolation and indifference. Try to engage in some activities that foster new conversation. Go to a movie, read a book together, watch a common show or sporting event together.

What is the balance in your joint marital bank account? I don't mean financially, although it is a good idea to assess that account, I mean your emotional bank account. The bank account that reflects the safety of your home. An account of trust instead of money. Can you trust the person that you married? Are they dependable? Are you? Is there an understanding between you both that help you know that you have each others best interest at heart? Are you both people of character? Do you sincerely apologize when you make a withdraw from the account? These are some questions to ask when assessing the condition of your foundation.

When I was a little girl, my grandfather was the vice president of the bank in town. He was well regarded as a man of character and considered trustworthy by all who knew him. He modeled many things for me but one thing that he instilled in me was a sense of taking care of the things that were important. He valued the importance of saving and that you didn't spend carelessly. He never bought a car on credit but was always saving for the next car he would own. Even though he made his living working for a bank he didn't want to give the bank money in the form of interest that he could save on his own. He modeled what it meant to have a bank account that was healthy and taught me that lesson early. He encouraged me to save 10 percent of my income. That meant if I made $10 I would save one of those dollars. The second dollar was to give away and feed my heart. To give to those in need or to the church. That was for the blessings that God provided for you. I could spend the rest. If I made $100 then ten of those dollars was to be saved. He also drove that lesson home by doubling whatever I put in my bank account. If I gave him $10 to put in my account then he would match that money and make a $20 deposit for me. I learned early the idea of return on your investment.

By investing in your family's emotional bank account you will see the dividends start to build. Take time to make more deposits than withdraws so that you can see your account in the black instead of in the red. Have a discussion about the importance of your account growing so that when a deposit is made you can address it right away by a simple statement such as "Wow, that deposit was a big one," when your spouse does something kind for you or an "Ouch, that withdrawal hurt," when perhaps forgetting an anniversary. The conversation become less attacking and more informative.

What are ways to add to your bank account? Take time for each other. Make a point of being in their presence not just present and anticipate your partner's needs. Focus on what is good about your relationship verses what is bad. Look at the big picture instead of focusing on the nitty gritty details that can rob you of your peace. What is positive in your home verses always focusing on the negative. Make today the day that your family begins with a new focus and looks to make each and every family member healthy. Something that a few of my friends failed to see when they were dealing with a bad marriage was that if their spouse failed, so did they. They were so busy tearing each other down that pretty soon everyone was bankrupt.

If your marriage has ended it can be a real challenge to move forward with your battle wounds and scars. Where do you put the hurt and disappointment that follows a broken marriage? Where do you store the bitterness that may follow? It is a real challenge to learn to "let go" of the emotions that may be part of your life.

One thing will always be true, and that is that you will forever be bound to your spouse because you have children together. You will both need to be present for weddings, Christenings, and birthday parties for grandkids. Let your focus be on self-healing. You will be forever scared by this breakup but don't allow the wound to continue to be open and festering and ultimately never heal. How do you do that? Ask God to use the "Balm of Gilead", a healing peace that surpasses all understanding. The ability to forgive and render grace (undeserved favor). Resolve to make peace because that ultimately leads to maturity.

When you got married, you choose a partner to share the journey with but that doesn't mean that you needed to completely lose yourself. If you identified strongly as a couple and suddenly find yourself back to being single you certainly are justified by being off balanced. The goal is to rediscover your footing. That takes some time but begin with baby steps that allow you to move forward. Sometimes I see couples so intent on knocking the other partner over that they don't realize that if that person falls so do you and you may take the kids with you.

Take a break from the hurt you feel and focus on what makes you feel fulfilled. What makes you happy? You were a complete person before you picked a partner to share the road with you. It's wonderful when that partnership works but when it doesn't you have a choice to make on how you will move forward. What tools do you need to sail your own boat? Take this moment to assess the condition of your life so that you can discover where there may be a need to do some balance readjustments. Do you have a support system that can help you? What is your prayer life like? Do you have other things in your life that fulfill you? Spend time rediscovering who you are and what are your passions.

If your marriage is still together but only hanging on by a thread, what can you do to stabilize it? How do you repair the damage that threatens to erode the foundation of your home? You need to gently and lovingly *"point up" (repair)* your family's foundation. What are the things that are eroding the foundation of your home? What baggage (anxiety) are you carrying around with you all day? Work, money, children, sex, etc. How about any baggage that you haven't let go of from your own childhood or past relationships. God longs to ease your burdens. "Be anxious for nothing ..." He longs to give you peace.

Let go and let God. Let go of your suitcase full of anxiety and let God carry it. Fix problems early by identifying what is damaging your home's foundation and address it before there is major damage.

When your home's foundation is cracking you need to look carefully at the causes. Is it water damage, or pressures from the structure? Can you carefully clean up the damage and point it up with mortar or do you need to reset the foundation? It is no different with your marriage. You need to identify the root cause of the damage. Is it an unresolved hurt, or the constant erosion of disrespect that is undermining your home's foundation? Once you identify the problem you can then address the repair. Take a look at how you resolve issues in your home in the past. Do you cleanse and lovingly fill in the faults of your spouse or do you chisel away at their flaw until there is a gaping hole, exposed for all to see? How does your spouse address your flaws? Sometimes when people share with me the struggles they are having in their marriage I can see them pull out the sledgehammer and begin pounding away at the very home they live in. They don't realize the damage they are doing to their homes by this attack on their spouse. Start today to "point up" the problem areas in your marriage and build up rather than tear down.

What are some of the trigger points that can damage your foundation?

Disrespect

Apathy …Not feeling valued

Lack of communication

Too much baggage

God not at the base of your foundation (building your home on sand verses a rock)

Start here … start now … to have the best marriage you can have. Build your home on a rock solid foundation.

Your Team Members … Once you stabilize and repair the foundation of your home you can then build on that structure. As any good team knows there are different skills and abilities that each member brings to the game. The same is true with a construction crew and it is vital for a successful outcome to know what each team member is capable of.

It is no different in a home. Your spouse, your parents, in-laws, siblings, and children all have their own unique makeup and abilities. It is important to gain eyes of understanding about whom these people are that you are sharing the journey with. You can then have an understanding of what they are capable of in the construction of your family home. If you see toxic behavior then that needs to be addressed before it can cause long-term damage to the home. You can't change another's behavior but you can certainly protect yourself from the damage that that toxic behavior can cause. Setting boundaries, learning how to communicate, and offering space sometimes are the best things that you can do to not let the damage that can so easily infiltrate your home from entering the front door. Cultivating homes of honor and respect can begin today by making it a priority. The goal is to bring out the best in each family member and to value the differences that each person brings to the table.

God (The Cornerstone) ... That all-important stone that serves as the first stone set in the foundation of a building. All other stones will be set in reference to this stone, thus determining the position of the entire structure. Allow God to be that stone in your home. Be sure to welcome God as He can bring stability to every aspect of your life. He also promises the gift of peace and we all could certainly use that in this noisy, troubled world.

The ultimate goal for yourself and your loved ones is to find peace. To experience peace in the middle of the storm is a challenge but as you grow in confidence, by having the tools you need, you can achieve that calmness no matter what the circumstances. As you gain wisdom you can appreciate the calm waters of life and see that as an opportunity to regroup, for you know that more storms will appear, it's just a matter of when ... and you want to be prepared.

The goal of your life is to gain in wisdom and maturity. To be a constant seeker of the attributes of integrity and to stand firmly, with confidence that you are a person of character. When that is achieved you will experience peace in all circumstances for you will know how to use the tools that you acquired to face the storms of life. You will feel empowered with the knowledge that you are on the right path.

Choose to maintain your integrity. Choose to let go of the past hurts and injustices not because the other person deserves it but because ultimately that is the only thing that you have control over. When you gain wisdom you will no longer be held captive by grudges and bitterness. You have let those negative emotions go and instead replace them with the gift of discernment: the ability to judge well; the ability to discern or understand what is a healthy relationship and what isn't. You will be able to see who is taking advantage of you and decide that maybe you need to avoid them. You will be able to understand when someone is robbing you of your peace and you can make a decision to not allow them to have that control over you. You relationships will begin to grow in health and as a result you will be healthier.

Goals (Maintenance) ... Now that you have done an assessment of your foundation, evaluated the strengths and weaknesses of your family members, and asked God to be the cornerstone of your home it is important to develop a maintenance schedule to keep your home healthy. One of the ways to do that is to establish goals for yourself, and your family. To identify where you are going and how do you get there. You will be able to refresh your marriage and bring life back into it if you see that it has staled through the years.

Don't look at this chapter of your life as what you have lost but look at it as an opportunity to reassess your life and grow just as your children are growing. I have many friends who are experiencing this chapter and I can assure you that they have come out the other side stronger and more aware of just who they are. They were so busy raising children that they forgot that they were also entitled to a life.

Look at this chapter as an opportunity to rediscover yourself and your spouse. What are some things that you want to achieve during this next chapter, such as vacations, developing new friends, expanding your mind, taking up a new hobby, or just taking some time to rest.

Take this opportunity to strengthen your marriage and look at it from God's point of view. We have to stop asking of marriage what God never designed it to give... perfect happiness, conflict-free living and a perfect spouse. We need to appreciate what God did design marriage to provide: partnership, spiritual intimacy and the ability to pursue God together. The scriptures tell us that we are to look to God for our fulfillment. We are to find our purpose and fulfillment in God and if we expect our spouse to fill that role he or she will fail every day. No person can live up to such high expectations. Everyone has bad days, yells at their spouse, or is downright selfish. Despite these imperfections, God created the husband and wife to compliment each other and steer each other in His direction. God created an "other-centered" union for a "me-centered" world. Living that way is a challenge!

The goals are to focus on your spouse's strengths rather than their weaknesses. To encourage rather than criticize and to pray for our spouse instead of gossiping about them. It is the goal of marriage to bring out the best in them and in the process it brings out the best in us.

I challenge my younger moms to find balance in their world so that they don't lose themselves along the journey. For the moms who are just entering this empty nest chapter, rest for a moment and regroup. The adjustments will come and then the opportunity for growth will present themselves, just keep your eyes open.

Whatever the circumstances, an empty nest is a new challenge. Walking past an empty room can leave you with a sense of loneliness and a need to reassess your purpose. First and foremost, be kind to yourself. Allow yourself the opportunity to grieve at the change in family dynamics and then allow time to become enlighten into what the next chapter will look like. Don't expect a quick fix but also don't allow anxiety to take over your life. Immerse yourself in self-discovery and don't be surprised if it takes time to gain that wisdom into discovering who you want to be. Ask God for guidance and wisdom and trust that he has great plans ahead for you.

CHAPTER 16
Enjoy The Ride

~

Parenting is one of the most challenging jobs there is. It comes with moments of joy and sorrow and a whole lot of emotions in between. It is a job whose goal is to work yourself out of that job. It is exhausting, challenging, and constant.

Now that you have completed this book and you are either feeling overwhelmed or empowered. I want you to pause. Take a moment to relax and realize that God picked you to raise these children that He entrusted you with. He knows what your skills are and He knows where you tend to fall short. You don't have to hide your shortcoming from God, He already knows all about you and He still picked you. So stop immediately if you feel overwhelmed. He wants to guide you and help you on this journey. He wants you to grow in wisdom right along with your kids.

When I teach the maternity orientation I always end with this observation. Labor is relatively short. You will spending about twenty four hours experiencing flu like symptoms. You are not really sure what your body is doing and you aren't sure how to respond. But once that labor is over there exists a thing of beauty, with a life all it's own. You have the privilege of witnessing a miracle and you had a part in participating in creation. Pause and enjoy that unbelievable moment. Don't let the stresses of labor blind you to the miracle before you. Likewise, don't let the trials of the journey as a parent blind you to the joys. Pause and take a moment to really look at parenthood from a Godly perspective.

God began this journey of creation by putting us in a perfect garden. Unfortunately, Adam and Eve took their eyes off of God and looked at what they didn't have, a piece of fruit from the tree of knowledge. God gave them all that they would need but He explained that there are some things that they weren't capable of knowing. They didn't have a full understanding of the whole picture of God and creation so for now they were given what they could comprehend. Then Satan came around and challenged that notion and cultivated unrest and doubt. When Adam and Eve took their eyes off of God they took a path to destruction, isolation and a feeling of loss. They tried to hide from God and experienced shame for the first time. The consequence for their actions was to be cast out of God's presence in the perfect garden and now they had to experience a world without God being physically present beside them. But God didn't desert them and He gave them a way for redemption. There were consequences for their actions but His love for them never floundered. He needed them to learn to turn from their self-centered ways and turn to a relationship with God that requires an understanding of who God is. He is our Savior and Redeemer. He is our Father and He calls us to repent and call out to Him. Just as we need to correct, discipline and guide our own children, God is doing the same with us. When you have a strong-willed child who is always challenging your authority and they want to do things their way, you can see that consequences for their actions may be the only way to teach them what is in their best interest. When you put restrictions on your children, such as don't eat candy before dinner or don't play in the street, it isn't that we don't love them and want to give them everything they want, it is that we do love them. Love is tough and sometimes tough love is required to bring about change.

God gives us a free-will and the freedom to choose if we want a relationship with Him or we want to travel on our own. When you have a guide beside you who knows the turns and the highs and lows of what we will be going through, then you can rest and trust that He will guide you accordingly. If you choose to go without this guide you may experience cliffs or take a path that leads you away from the mark and not toward it. The choice is yours, but rest assured that God wants you to choose Him!

He can give you wisdom, discernment, and joy along the journey. He will bring you comfort and purpose and a sense of what the big picture looks like. He, unfortunately, can't bring you on an obstacle-free journey. Wouldn't it be nice if that was the gift for believing in God, but the purpose of your life is to travel the journey. To experience the highs and lows of life and to share that journey with others who are experiencing their own struggles. But the one thing that God will provide over and over again is His peace. Peace during the storms, peace during your moments of greatest loss and greatest joys. Peace when you're tired and alone, peace when you're feeling battered by the storms of life.

I know how tough life is, my teenage years were riddled with heavy burdens that I would have to experience. My parents divorced during my sophomore year of high school, my mom remarried my junior year and my sister Kathy died of kidney failure six days before her kidney transplant during my senior year. The ground under my feet was shaken multiple times and yet my faith was cultivated and I felt God's presence through the storms. It wasn't easy but I kept my eyes on God and not my circumstances. I felt His peace.

I don't know your circumstances or whether your faith was cultivated as a child or nonexistent. Many of you may be overwhelmed by the scripture that I listed or have never even cracked the binding of a Bible so that it is completely foreign to you. Rest in the knowledge that God isn't going to quiz you on how well you know the Apostles, or if you know where to find the story of creation in the Bible. He wants a relationship with you and He wants you to talk to Him. It doesn't have to be a fancy prayer, just sit down and talk heart to heart, He is a good listener.

If you ever studied the Apostles, you got to see that they weren't these holy men who had great knowledge of the scripture, but they were ordinary rough-and-tumbled men. Four were fishermen, one was a tax collector, some were bold and brass, and others were quiet and reserved. What was true with all of them was that they were willing to be taught and transformed. They were teachable and used that wisdom to transform the world. They didn't always understand and they needed to be redirected many times but God had a vision for them and He slowly allowed them to see that vision in themselves. All except one became passionate believers who stood tall during the storms that would come. Judas didn't trust what God's plan was and turned away. He looked to his own needs instead of God's vision. He made the choice to go down a path that was alone and isolated and the result was tragic. God wants better for you. He believes in you and already put His trust in you. Now it is time for you to trust Him and believe in yourself.

Parenting is a challenge but there is no job that is more important. No matter what stage you are at with raising your child, don't let the trials and dramas blind you to the fact that you are watching up close and personal a person develop. Learn to embrace each chapter, even the challenging ones, because before you know it they will be ready to leave home.

Let's review what you have learned. That God is calling you to be a lighthouse for your children. To be that tall object that shines its beacon and guides your children to safety. The lighthouse stands alone and its light is always shining. It is cared for by an attentive keeper who knows all about the structure and works diligently to keep it in good repair. Its light shines during the brightest days and the darkest nights. That is what God's plan is for you in blessing you with His children. He wants you to guide them on their journey and take care of yourself so that your light is always able to shine. He wants you to be attentive so that you can keep them from harm. Your job is to be the lighthouse and your child's job is to learn to sail their own boat.

It is a real challenge to educate our children on how to manage their own boat. It takes time and patience to equip them with the skills that they will need to navigate their own vessel. It is important to educate them on what they will need for their journey. Their life-saver, a compass, and their anchor. These tools will assist them and keep them safe when the storms of life come their way. All of our teachings needs to be done in the calm moments of our lives when the message can be heard. It is vital to assemble a team that can assist during the journey and important to know where the challenges are such as rocky shores or strong currents that may damage their small boat.

Don't take everything too seriously and bring laughter and joy into the home. You aren't going to get everything right but as long as the overall tone in your home is positive, you are doing okay. Build memories, develop traditions, and cultivate their faith. Have a home where everyone feels safe and the porch light is always shining.

Help you children to become independent, self-sufficient, responsible adults so that one day they can set out, away from the safe harbor of home, to discover the world on their own. And when times get tough, call out to God. Just as you want your kids to trust you, know that you can trust your Heavenly Father in the same way. Now put your faith to action.

CPSIA information can be obtained
at www.ICGtesting.com
Printed in the USA
LVHW022343270521
688666LV00033B/782